GOD'S ORDER

ORDER IN THE CHURCH AND PULPIT

*To Br. Britton
God bless you
always. Keep the
faith.*

*Pastor Heppin
2011*

GOD'S ORDER

ORDER IN THE CHURCH AND PULPIT

DR. WILLIAM E. FLIPPIN, SR.

Mall Publishing Co.
THE PRINTED WORD THE PLANTED SEED

HIGHLAND PARK, ILLINOIS

Copyright © 2007 Dr. William E. Flippin, Sr.

Printed in the United States of America

Published by:
Mall Publishing
641 Homewood Avenue
Highland Park, Illinois 60035
877.203.2453

Cover and text design by Marlon Villadiego.

All rights reserved. No part of this book may be reproduced or transmitted in any form or by any means, graphic, electronic, or mechanical, including photocopying, recording, taping, or by any information storage or retrieval system, without the permission in writing from the publisher.

ISBN: 1-934165-17-4

For licensing / copyright information, for additional copies or for use in specialized settings contact:

The Pearls of Great Price Ministries of Georgia, Inc.
4919 Flatshoals Pkwy
Suite 201, Box 203
Decatur, Georgia 30034
www.thepearlsofgreatprice.com

CONTENTS

DEDICATION vii

ACKNOWLEDGEMENTS ix

INTRODUCTION xi

PART ONE: ORDER IN THE CHURCH

CHAPTER ONE:
Defining the Problem 3

CHAPTER TWO:
The Roots of the Problem 25

CHAPTER THREE:
Confronting the Problem 39

PART TWO: ORDER IN THE PULPIT

CHAPTER FOUR:
Seeking the Vision 91

CHAPTER FIVE:
Laying the Foundation 99

CHAPTER SIX:
Answering the Call 111

CHAPTER SEVEN:
Practical Matters 123

CONCLUSION:
The Verdict 133

ABOUT THE AUTHOR 137

DEDICATION

This book is dedicated with love to my wife,
Sylvia Taylor Flippin
and my mother
Virginia Brooks Flippin
(1909-1989).

ACKNOWLEDGEMENTS

This current project is a fresh look and revision written with twenty-five years of pastoral service. Additionally, as a forty-year member and active participant of the church, we submit this work.

Special thanks and appreciation to the Rev. Dr. Michael Brewer and to my son who serves as the Executive Assistant to the Senior Pastor, the Rev. Richard C. Flippin. This project could never have been completed without the teamwork of The Greater Piney Grove Baptist Church and our dedicated church staff. Thanks to Charlene Ross and Tangie Black for your dedication and **push**.

To the church of my youth, The Fifteenth Avenue Baptist Church, Nashville, Tennessee, where I received early Christian training and development that will always inform my life and ministry.

To Dr. John H. Corbitt, former Director of the National BSU Retreat, where I served as a National President in 1974, and also to the late Mrs. Irene Grinstead Turner who nurtured me through the Baptist Student Union at Fisk University.

To the late Dr. Edward R. Davie, who gave me my first opportunity to serve in professional ministry through the Georgia Baptist Convention.

INTRODUCTION

Books are written with many intentions. However, the best books are written to provoke our thinking. *GOD'S ORDER: Order in the Church and Pulpit* is in that genre. The essence is simple. The message is—Mind your manners, you're in His house. Dr. William E. Flippin Sr., Pastor of The Greater Piney Grove Baptist Church writes this book from years of careful observation of the erosion of church decorum.

I have written elsewhere of the Scriptural warning against casting "your pearls before swine" (Matthew 7:6). This book reminds us of one interpretation of that verse. Swine will trample our pearls and then turn on us, making us look like we're the bad guys. If the same Scripture were written in a modern translation for leaders, it might say, "Don't cast your vision in front of the bottom twenty percent because they're going to destroy your vision and turn on you."

I am not calling a group of people names, but we must be strategic in our casting. In order for our message to find open ears and ready hearts in the church, it is essential for today's congregations to recover an atmosphere of decorum, respect, and dignity.

Regardless of your church background, you do have standards. The corporate community calls it SOP (Standard Operating Procedures). These are relevant, communicated clearly, enforced rigorously for a reason—because this defines corporate culture for that organization.

ALL RISE: Order in the Church reminds and informs us that there is still need for order in the church. Dr. Flippin not only diagnoses the problem of disrespect and disorder, he also prescribes the cure. For the good of the church, I hope the pearls of wisdom in this book will find enthusiastic readers.

Samuel R. Chand, D.D.
President, Samuel Chand
Chancellor, Beulah Heights University
Atlanta, Georgia

PART ONE:
ORDER IN THE CHURCH

1
DEFINING THE PROBLEM

IN THE BEGINNING, ORDER!

Creation came into existence through and by divine order. The alternative to order is chaos and confusion, the domain of the devil. According to the first book of Moses, the earth was without form and void before God imposed the divine will upon the unshaped chaos. The Spirit of God brooded upon the waste and emptiness, determining the plan for an orderly universe. Darkness was upon the face of the deep, but at God's command light appeared

> THE SPIRIT OF GOD BROODED UPON THE WASTE AND EMPTINESS, DETERMINING THE PLAN FOR AN ORDERLY UNIVERSE.

and from that moment the creation began to align itself with the order of God's purpose. Light distinguished itself from darkness. Day and night took shape and time began.

God determined the architecture of existence, creating the vault of the heavens and separating water from land. At the right time, life appeared and the Creator endowed each creature with the ability to reproduce itself according to its own kind. Cherry trees would not beget acorns, nor dogs give birth to cats. In every realm of creation, God established the orderly patterns that rule the universe. God looked upon His carefully planned handiwork and pronounced the creation good.

God does not act chaotically or randomly. The Creator has a blueprint for our lives and our world. Even in apparent tension and turmoil, God speaks and operates in order. Through the orderly creativity of God, that which is nothing becomes something. Unfortunately, chaos and disorder still exist in the world, and these forces seek to undermine God's good purposes. Sometimes disorder sows the seeds of confusion even within the church.

THE CHANGING CHURCH

Since beginning my ministry many years ago in Tennessee, I have seen drastic changes sweep through the church. Many of those changes have been positive and productive. Nonetheless, other changes adopted in the name of progress disconnected God's people from one another and from cherished traditions of Christian conduct and behavior.

I have been privileged to serve as senior pastor of three great churches. Although these congregations differed in locale, size, and setting, all shared a common need for leadership development. If we are to regain a sense of appropriate decorum in today's church, we must train a generation of leaders to maintain order. Far too often, I hear ministers and church leaders bemoaning, "Today's members do not know how to act in the church."

We give thanks that many sincere and active members of our churches today are first-generation Christians. We rejoice that God has drawn these men and women into the body of Christ. Yet Jesus warns us that it is difficult to place new wine in old wine skins without causing a mess—and I have seen that mess first-hand when new believers try to settle into the old, traditional patterns of church behavior.

We don't want to worship the past, but many practices developed within the church through the centuries are just as relevant and important today as in former generations. "Tradition" is considered a bad word in some circles, but our parents and great-great-grandparents had good reasons for many of the habits they cultivated. I am amused now as I find myself not only recalling but actually reciting the wise old tales my parents uttered as they reared us. At the time, I thought they were out of their minds. The passing years have radically changed my perspective on the value of tradition and accumulated wisdom.

> "TRADITION" IS CONSIDERED A BAD WORD IN SOME CIRCLES...

SEPARATING THE WHEAT FROM THE CHAFF

By trial and error, and often through painful mistakes, earlier generations of Christians forged faithful and sound ways to worship and serve God. The inherited wisdom of those who earlier walked the path of discipleship enriches and blesses us. Discarding the lessons learned by those struggling saints is folly. We welcome changes when those changes are God-inspired, but how foolish we are to scorn "that old time religion" just so we can chase after the latest fad in fashion or behavior. In the words of the old adage, why should this generation of worshipers set out to re-invent the wheel?

Table 1

Behavior	Traditional	Post Traditional	Modern/Contemporary
Dress Code			
Worship/Prayers			
Readings			
Songs/Hymns			
Sermon Style			
Etc.			
Reflect similarities and differences as a comparison for change.			

Yet the church is accidentally discarding priceless traditions because we lack a structured process to train and equip the total church. We will not accomplish discipleship training through sporadic seminars and retreats. Nor can we rely entirely upon membership in a Sunday School class. Discipleship training must be an ongoing process embedded in the corporate life of the church. Most African American churches master in planning events, but after a big celebration or anniversary the cycle ends until next year. We must develop strategies and processes that will disciple men and women to witness and to work throughout the year.

I sometimes think of the Christian faith as an old-time bucket brigade. Before the days of fire-trucks and hydrants, when a building blazed the whole community rallied with buckets. Creating a human chain, firefighters passed water hand-to-hand from the nearest river or pond. Every bucket mattered. Each person in the chain played a crucial role. If some citizens abandoned their work, the chain was broken and the precious water failed to reach the fire.

In the same way, the message and the values of Christianity pass from person to person and from one generation to another. If the chain is broken—if a single generation fumbles the mission—how will the treasure of our faith reach our children's children? We must shoulder the responsibility to maintain our traditions and implement the training programs to bequeath our values and customs to the future. The present paradigm shift of worship and church polity sends a signal that in the past we were wrong or unbiblical. The dilemma is real when we look for "a new thing" and discard the old. We can maintain some worthwhile traditions without becoming "traditional."

> WE CAN MAINTAIN SOME WORTHWHILE TRADITIONS WITHOUT BECOMING "TRADITIONAL."

Through this book I intend to clarify the crucial need for order in today's church and to suggest steps for combating the confusion invading our congregations. No one can entirely transcend his own particular tradition. I won't pretend to do so, nor would I want to. I write from my perspective within the black Baptist church, but I write to brothers and sisters in the church at large. I hope my thoughts and ideas will serve congregations and ministers in all denominations, traditions, and church structures.

All of us share a common calling from Christ, a calling that lays claim on our lives individually and collectively. In obedience to that calling, we need a clear understanding of our responsibility and roles. The harvest is plentiful, but the laborers are few. The preaching and sharing of God's Word and the leading of God's people must be accomplished through the love of God. This book is written humbly and lovingly to encourage and to instruct the body of Christ.

TRAINING FOR LEADERSHIP

We believe that each church member, associate minister, and leader in the local church can grow into a fruitful and successful ministry. However, that growth requires guidance and training along the way.

> How can we hold our people accountable...

Young Christians and novice ministers frequently confess a lack of clarity regarding their roles and responsibilities. With solid training and instruction, we could correct or avoid entirely many mistakes in etiquette and missteps in worship. How can we hold our people accountable to standards of behavior if they haven't been properly instructed? In many of our churches, we have made minimal attempts to address these errors by offering to teach church rules and behavior in youth retreats, church directories and new member orientation classes. None of these have gone quite far enough.

Unfortunately, too often in our churches the members and leaders most in need of training and information are absent and excuse themselves from these sessions. We must stress our expectation that training and teaching opportunities are essential for Christian growth. If Jesus submitted himself to the weekly teaching of God's word in the synagogue, surely we too must maintain and humble and teachable hearts.

Church leaders have impressed upon me the need to expand my first book and give a clear standard as an aid in improving church behavior and etiquette. Let us rise to the task of carefully reviewing the foundations of decency and order in the church. In earlier works, I have asserted that there is an unwritten church code of behavior that members are expected to know and follow. We might think of this standard of behavior as an unwritten set of "Ten Commandments."

Chapter One • *Defining the Problem*

Sometimes we can find these traditions and customs in the word of God. Unfortunately the people of God have often resisted lofty standards. For instance, when Moses returned from Mount Sinai with the Ten Commandments carved upon two stone tablets, he found that the people had already turned away from decency and given themselves to idol worship and carousing. "So Moses' anger became hot, and he cast the tablets out of his hands and broke them at the foot of the mountain." (Exodus 32:19) Only after great effort, suffering, and repentance are the law tablets restored to disobedient Israel.

> THE CHURCH REQUIRES ORDER

Can we glimpse the modern church in this ancient story? Has our continued disobedience and ignorance shattered the tablets containing the commandments of decency and reverence? We must clearly communicate these rules, norms, and expectations to each new generation of believers. Our expectations must be so clear and compelling that no one can plead ignorance. As the Lord commanded the prophet Habakkuk, "Write the vision and make it plain on tablets, that he may run who reads it." (Habakkuk 2:2)

The church requires order and we, as church leaders, must implement and restore this order in our congregations. The task may not be easy, but much is at stake. This is our calling and our challenge. As motivational expert John Maxwell reminds us, everything rises and falls on leadership.

THE EROSION OF RESPECT

The contemporary church cannot casually assume that individuals know the expectations and requirements for responsible participation in congregational life and worship. We teach that the Holy Spirit will guide the believer into all truth, but that doctrine does not excuse the shoddy training and slipshod standards that encourage disorder and misbehavior in the body of Christ. Church members too often behave in a manner that neither dignifies nor reveres the kingdom of God. We live in a time of growing disrespect for the House of Worship and for those who serve the Lord's people and the institutional church.

How can we account for the waning esteem of once respected institutions in the church? Several factors have contributed to this unhappy situation during the past few decades.

One serious issue is the national and global climate of diminished trust in leaders and authority figures of any kind. The erosion of trust in our leaders became obvious during the divisiveness of the Viet Nam War and the national crisis of President Nixon's Watergate cover-up. Since those days media reporters scouting for the next juicy scandal have spotlighted one national embarrassment after another. The press and television constantly assail the American public with lurid stories of leaders who have fallen short.

Consider:
- the 34 year-old teacher who went to prison for her clandestine relationship with a 12 year old boy in her class;
- the televangelist who funneled ministry donations into his own pocket for such an opulent lifestyle that even his dog lounged in an air-conditioned dog house;
- the repeated steroid-abuse charges leveled at national sports heroes;
- the cities inflamed by allegations that police officers misuse their authority in dealing with minorities;
- the unseemly account of an American President's intimate relations with a White House intern;
- the sad spectacle of American soldiers' court-martialed for abusing and humiliating prisoners of war.

No wonder the average person is suspicious of authority figures.

Chapter One • *Defining the Problem*

The erosion of trust has progressed so far that today all public figures are suspect. A President is considered popular and successful if only 40% of the American people disapprove of his work.

A recent survey of American opinion found that roughly one fourth of those polled felt police officers are untrustworthy. Physicians were even less trusted. About 70% of those questioned stated their distrust of lawyers and government officials. Religious leaders don't fare well, either. A little over one fourth of those polled distrusted Protestant ministers and nearly one half said that Catholic priests are untrustworthy.

The reasons for the decline of trust are many and varied. We might point to generational values, historical factors, or the overzealous scrutiny of the press. At the end of the day, how we got into this situation is irrelevant. What matters is that our culture has a built-in bias against institutions, government, leaders, and public servants.

To be clear, I am not saying that we have experienced a wholesale failure of leadership in our country. Many leaders are honest and selfless servants of the people. The point I'm making has to do with perception. Whether justified or not, John Q. Public devoutly believes that most leaders have ulterior motives and hidden agendas. This persistent doubt undermines the effectiveness of leadership in general, since leaders rely upon the trust of their constituents. In a self-fulfilling prophecy, this distrust discourages qualified and honorable people from running for office. I have observed a similar reluctance to enter the ministry.

> CONGREGATIONS ARE CRIPPLED BY POWER STRUGGLES OVER ISSUES OF TRADITION, CHANGE, MORALITY, AND AUTHORITY.

DISTRUST IN THE CHURCH

If anything, the climate of distrust is even more pronounced in the church. In twenty-five years of ministry I have served three congregations and visited many more in traveling around the nation. Sadly, I have seen a similar scenario play out again and again. Congregations are crippled by power struggles over issues of tradition, change, morality, and authority. Inevitably the pastor gets caught in the crossfire in these feuds. Ministerial motives may be impugned, integrity challenged, and personalities dragged through the mud.

In such bitter circumstances, countless ministers are miserable and uncertain of their calling. Citing thirty-five years of church consultation, workshop leadership, and information gathering, Lyle Schaller flatly states that there are more unhappy pastors than ever before in American history. The causes of this unhappiness are many and varied, but prominent among the problems that pastors bemoan are brief, rotating-door ministries; low attendance; poor participation; lack of lay leadership; unclear goals and expectations in ministry; congregations obsessed with institutional survival; and increased competition between churches.

One thing is certain: unhappy pastors lead to unhappy churches. Ironically, the more a congregation mistreats its pastor, the more likely the church will suffer indirectly as the minister loses enthusiasm and excitement. In other words, the mistrust of pastors is harmful not only to those who stand in the pulpit, but also to the people in the pews. Pastors and flocks are in the church together and one cannot be happy at the expense of the other. As the prophet Hosea warns, "And it shall be: like people, like priest." (Hosea 4:9)

In some circles, the general atmosphere of distrust translates into blatant disregard for the church and its leadership. Efforts to raise the standards of behavior and conduct in the church arouse suspicion and skepticism because leaders aren't respected. In part, this

Chapter One • *Defining the Problem*

accounts for the church's acceptance of the contemporary philosophy that anything and everything is appropriate and proper. With the adoption of a come-as-you-are attitude and the norm of casual dress in local churches, we have sent a signal that contemporary Christians recognize no boundaries of proper dress, conduct, or behavior.

LIBERTY MISUSED

The New Testament teaches us that the Spirit of God brings liberation to the people of Christ. "For you, brethren, have been called to liberty; only do not use liberty as an opportunity for the flesh, but through love serve one another." (Galatians 5:13). Some seize upon that wonderful doctrine and twist it to suit themselves, claiming that anything goes.

> WE HAVE PERVERTED CHRISTIAN LIBERTY INTO PERSONAL LICENSE…

Are we to believe that freedom in Christ allows us to act in any manner we choose? Are there no limits or boundaries given to those who follow the Lord? One tragic outcome of this misguided thinking is the rise of divorce in the church. Lackluster commitments tear our families apart. Like the larger society in which we live, the church is losing its sense of firm values and moral fiber.

Again consider Paul's words: "For you, brethren, have been called to liberty; *only do not use liberty as an opportunity for the flesh, but through love serve one another.*" (Galatians 5:13, emphasis added) We have perverted Christian liberty into personal license, as if standards of conduct and behavior no longer apply in the church. We have bought into the cultural notion that the only guidelines in life are me, myself and I. Whatever I want to do, whatever is comfortable to me, whatever suits my values—that is how I will live my life. Never mind the traditions of the church. Forget the teaching of Scripture. Down with leaders who try to tell me how to live my life.

The apostle Paul was wise to warn us against turning freedom into self-indulgence. Are we wise enough to heed the warning?

This book focuses on church etiquette, leadership, and order in the church. In lay terms, how do Christians act, particularly in the church? What are the do's and don'ts of public worship? How do those outside the congregation perceive the church? What are we doing to help train new members who have no prior Christian experience? Have we taken too far the modern approach to church growth that allows people to "come as they are"? The Old Testament law is specific, but what about the New Testament? Does Scripture impose no limitations or guidelines for those who walk by faith and not by sight? What does grace require? Are Christians accountable for the unspoken witness of our deeds and our behavior in the eyes of the world? Other world religions demand a standard of behavior, offering guidelines for the world to emulate. Does God's rich grace give Christians an excuse to lag behind other religions in our conduct?

MINISTERIAL ETIQUETTE

While in seminary, I enrolled in Bishop Nolan B. Harmon's course on ministerial etiquette. At that time, in the early 1980's, Bishop Harmon was in his nineties but that venerable churchman still had a keen and insightful mind. Many students registered for the class with minimal expectations, assuming that the instructor was past his prime and out of step with the times. We didn't voice our doubts aloud, but some of us wondered what this old man could teach young seminary students. As beginning pastors who had been raised in and around the church, surely we knew all the ins and outs of ministerial etiquette.

I signed up for the class, anticipating an easy A and knowing the course would look good on my transcript. Studying under someone with the reputation of Bishop Harmon would be a point of pride in years to come. After all, the Bishop had served the church ably for decades. His academic prowess was evident in his prestigious editorial work on The Interpreters Bible released in the 1950's. He had even corresponded with Martin Luther King, Jr. during the most tumultuous days of the civil rights movement, prompting Dr. King's 1963 "Letter from the Birmingham Jail." The class would give me the opportunity to make the acquaintance of a prominent Christian leader, even if I already knew everything about pastoral conduct.

Wow! Was I wet behind the ears! The first thing I learned in that course was how much I didn't know. What a blessing to learn pastoral propriety first-hand from a veteran practitioner. What we received in that classroom came from no textbook. Bishop Harmon didn't bore us with abstract ideas and impractical notions.

> ...THE CHURCH IS MEANT TO BE THE HEADLIGHTS...

Instead, he shared from the deep well of personal experience. He passed along to us the substance of ministerial behavior as others had passed that vital message on to him.

Using his wisdom and hard-earned experience, Bishop Harmon forced us to examine ourselves. He challenged us to make certain our lives, integrity, and character would not shame the church and the Christian ministry. Under his inspiring guidance, we resolved to conduct ourselves honorably and respectably in order to glorify our Lord and elevate our calling.

Over twenty years later I find myself often referring to the insightful lectures of Bishop Harmon. Thankfully remembering his tutelage and reflecting upon my own years of pastoral practice, I have developed this book on Christian etiquette. Both those who sit in the pews and those who rise to the pulpit may find helpful council in these pages. I humbly offer this book to the church at large, trusting God will use it to bless and build up the beloved family of Christ.

DRIVING WITHOUT HEADLIGHTS

The late Dr. Martin Luther King, Jr. invoked a vivid image to reveal the gap between the high calling of the church and the disappointing practice of the church. In a powerful sermon, Dr. King argued that the church is meant to be the headlights of the world, providing guidance and clear leadership toward God's Kingdom. In fact, Dr. King observed, the church is too often content to be the taillights for society. Instead of boldly pointing the way in hope, Christianity settles for bringing up the rear, more led than leading. As a result, human culture wanders in the dark, while the church ineffectually hitches a ride, following rather than setting the trends of society.

> THE CHURCH BELONGS TO GOD.

A weary colleague recently confessed, "I am so tired of hot dog evangelism."

When asked what he meant, he explained, "The church has adopted the tactics of the local supermarket that gives away free hotdogs to attract customers. We will do anything to get people through the church doors. We lower our standards, offer social incentives, and turn our worship services into entertainment events. Worship has become, "Lights! Camera! Action!" Once we get people inside the building, we condone any kind of behavior in order to keep them there. We make no demands that might diminish our attendance figures."

He shook his head sadly.

"I was called to be a minister," he said. "I never meant to be a hot dog vendor."

I understand his discouragement. We have set the bar so low that any attempt to establish standards for church behavior sparks indignant protests. Sadly, some Christians have the attitude that church is the one place nobody can tell them what to do.

Chapter One • *Defining the Problem*

"It's my church and I pay my money," they say. "I can do whatever I want to in my church."

Such statements betray a childish misunderstanding of the true nature of Christianity. The church doesn't belong to the members. Neither does the church belong to the deacons, the choir or even the minister. The church belongs to God. When we arrive for worship, we enter God's house and God has every right to expect us to conduct ourselves according to God's holy standards.

When visiting someone else's home, would you have the audacity to prop your feet on the coffee table, to spill food on the sofa, and to change the station while your host was engrossed in a television show? Of course not! When visiting an acquaintance we honor their space and maintain our best behavior. If the host greets me at the door and asks me to remove my shoes before treading on the newly-refinished hardwood floors, I comply gladly as a sign of respect. If I cannot do so, I leave.

What about our respect for God's space? We have lost the sense of awe and humility that Moses showed when he removed his sandals before the burning bush. "Now Moses was tending the flock of Jethro his father-in-law, the priest of Midian. And he led the flock to the back of the desert, and came to Horeb, the mountain of God. And the Angel of the LORD appeared to him in a flame of fire from the midst of a bush. So he looked, and behold, the bush was burning with fire, but the bush was not consumed. Then Moses said, 'I will now turn aside and see this great sight, why the bush does not burn.' So when the LORD saw that he turned aside to look, God called to him from the midst of the bush and said, 'Moses, Moses!' And he said, 'Here I am.' Then He said, 'Do not draw near this place. Take your sandals off your feet, for the place where you stand is holy ground.' Moreover He said, 'I am the God of your father—the God of Abraham, the God of Isaac, and the God of Jacob.' And Moses hid his face, for he was afraid to look upon God." (Exodus 3:1-6)

Moses knew he was in the presence of God and he was eager to honor God's requirements. Surely when we gather in church the living God is as truly present there as in the burning bush. Where is our humility, our respect, and our readiness to meet God's standards of behavior?

CUES FROM THE CULTURE

I observe these lowered standards in many areas of our culture. For instance, the local malls and shopping centers are thronged with young men and women who socialize with no pretense of shopping. The malls in our communities offer weekend parties of styling and profiling for young and old. The shopping mall has become the meeting and greeting place for our youth. Some argue that at least this keeps youngsters off the streets. Consequently, to keep the malls full, we allow people to gather who have no intentions of shopping. Thus we undermine the whole purpose of the mall so that we won't offend or turn anyone away.

Likewise, to keep the schools full we allow students to attend classes without the required tools for learning. Pupils arrive empty-handed for class, without texts, pencils, or notebooks. Even worse, students file into school with absolutely no intention of learning. We tolerate disobedience, disrespect, disruptive behavior, and outright violence from our youngsters. As long as students show up, schools condone practically any conduct.

In the same misguided spirit, in order to keep the church full we welcome men, women, boys, and girls who come with no intention of worshiping or meeting God. The House of Prayer becomes a house of socializing, a house of fashion shows, a house of gossip, a house of passing the time, a house no longer ruled by the Master of the family.

When personal freedom is carried to the extreme, each person insists on the right to do his or her own thing without regard to

Chapter One • *Defining the Problem*

others. This kind of unrestrained freedom leads to disorder and chaos. No responsible parent will say to a child, "Do whatever you want. I don't care." God loves us too much to let us run wild without guidelines or restraints. This is especially true in church. When the standards of behavior are trampled underfoot, the church suffers as a result.

On the other hand, the church is not a place where a few leaders boss everyone else, making endless rules just to prove who's in charge. As we will see in later discussion, true leadership is not dictatorship. Christians in general, and black Christians in particular, encounter the powers of oppression at every level of life. The church should be a refuge of liberation.

This is the challenge before the church: to provide an atmosphere of freedom, and yet to celebrate that freedom within God-given guidelines of respect, reverence, and mutual affection. Too much liberty leads to anarchy and confusion. Too little freedom leads to staleness and oppression. I envision a middle way that acknowledges our spiritual freedom from the coercive structures of a fallen world and also practices the joyful reverence and obedience that we owe to our Lord and Savior. I hunger both for order based on fairness and justice and for the respectful freedom that encourages us to offer our very best to Christ.

A LESSON FROM THE COURTROOM

My inspiration for this vision is the American courtroom. Various circumstances require a pastor to appear in court. I've stood before the judge many times to provide character references, defense, and support for someone on trial. Although I have made numerous court appearances, I always approach the courtroom with an edge of anxiety. One doesn't stroll casually into a court of law. Armed guards and metal detectors screen all incoming visitors. If one accompanies a prisoner approaching from the jail, the security is even more intense—additional guards, careful scrutiny, manacles on the prisoner, and a series of locking doors and barred gates that make the freedom of the outside world feel like a dim memory.

The importance of this security is underlined by the sad events that unfolded on March 11, 2005 in a Fulton County courtroom in Atlanta, Georgia when a defendant overpowered a guard and seized her gun. Brandishing the gun, the man held hostage everyone in the courtroom. Before making his escape, the criminal shot and killed both the judge and the court stenographer. On his way out of the building he added another victim to the list when he lethally wounded a pursuing deputy.

> THE CONTEST BETWEEN PROSECUTION AND DEFENSE...

How did this tragedy happen? Sloppy courtroom security is partly to blame. Given the terrible outcome, the need for proper behavior and strict standards in court is painfully clear. In the aftermath of the killings new security doors and metal detectors have been installed in the courthouse along with tightened procedural guidelines.

Another culprit in those courtroom murders is the erosion of respect for law and justice. Bad enough that the accused man would escape from trial, but the wanton and pointless killing of court officials reveals his utter contempt for all that represents the law. If the basic foundation stones of our culture are so flagrantly attacked, how long can our country stand?

Perhaps I am out of step with our times because I bring a respectful attitude to the courtroom. I have no reason to be afraid of our legal system. Just for the record, I've never been the person wearing handcuffs! Yet every time I find myself in court, I feel a tingle of fearful respect. I am impressed by the unyielding power of the court and the terrible outcome of running afoul of the judicial

Chapter One • *Defining the Problem*

process. In the presence of that authority, I feel something akin to the biblical notion of the fear of the Lord: mingled awe, respect, humility, and deference.

Confronted by the furnishings and symbols of the court, most visitors drop their voices upon entering the room and adopt their best behavior. Hats come off. Cell phones and pagers are silenced. Flippant comments die on the lips, and conduct is respectful. The courtroom setting is designed to purposely arouse such feelings.

When I enter the court I see the tables set aside for opposing counsel. The contest between prosecution and defense reminds me of the combat between truth and falsehood, the profound battle waged between law and criminality. The courtroom is

> THE COURTROOM AND THE HOUSE OF WORSHIP ARE SO SIMILAR

the scene of an ongoing struggle reaching back to the beginnings of recorded history, a struggle of eternal significance in which choices, decisions, and deeds are weighed in the balance.

My eyes survey the flags in proud array. Those symbolic banners represent the ascending authority of county, state, and one nation under God. The issues addressed in the courtroom reach beyond those walls and shape the direction of our culture. Matters decided today make the future our children will inherit. The seat reserved for the court reporter symbolizes this larger dimension of the judicial process. In a sense, the eyes of the world keep watch in the courtroom, eager to see justice done and ready to learn from judicial wisdom.

The jury box assures me that the events of the court are not reserved for the high and mighty. Ordinary people play a part in this drama. My neighbors and peers bring their best gifts to the service of the court, sacrificing their time and energy in a higher cause.

The bailiff and uniformed guards symbolize the court's power to establish justice and maintain order. When the judge enters through the massive doors, the bailiff does not request but demands, "ALL RISE!" Everyone jolts upright and faces the judge as they approach their seat on a platform symbolically raised above the rest of the room. The judge wears a black robe, the visible sign representing both authority and years of fervent preparation. A hush descends and no one moves until the judge announces, "You may be seated."

If one dares to show disrespect or scorn, the court defends its own dignity swiftly and decisively. The officers of the court condone no comments or deeds that demean or belittle the judicial system. The wise visitor to the court follows the rules, abides by the guidelines, and conducts himself courteously. The unwise who show contempt will find themselves fined, jailed, or ejected from the room.

THE COURTROOM AND THE CHURCH SANCTUARY

- The judge and the clergy are both robed to set their respective offices apart for dignity and deference.
- The judge and the clergy exercise authority, one backed by Constitution and government, the other empowered by the Word of God and the Holy Spirit.
- The judge speaks and all listen; likewise the preacher in the pulpit demands our full attention.
- The judge announces judgments that affect lives for years to come; the preacher delivers a gospel that affects lives for eternity.

The courtroom and the house of worship are so similar, but where is the respect and reverence due to the church? I see an assault to discredit and challenge the authority, the decisions, and the God-ordained responsibility of the clergy and the church. If we conducted ourselves in a court of law as many worshipers behave in our churches, the judge would charge us with contempt and the bailiff would forcibly escort us from the room.

Although contemptuous and disrespectful conduct is not universal in the church, many congregations have come to accept an almost qualified and dignified disorder. If God so clearly valued order in the very fabric of creation, then the church for which Christ died must also honor a divinely appointed order.

> "THERE MUST BE ORDER IN THE CHURCH!"

If the Judge of all flesh suddenly decided to enforce the standards of the courtroom within the church, many congregational leaders and members would be handcuffed and charged with contempt, confusion, and disorderly conduct. The time has come for ministers and leaders to stand up as God's bailiffs and issue the stern cry: **"There must be order in the church!"**

2

THE ROOTS OF THE PROBLEM

THE COSTS OF CONFLICT

For over ten years, I had the honor of serving in the Department of Black Church Relations for the Georgia Baptist Convention. In that role I provided leadership training and resources for both fledgling congregations and established, growing churches. I also intervened in congregational conflicts. These conflicts almost always grew out of power struggles to determine who was in charge of the church.

Even the healthiest congregations sometimes experience conflict. In fact, some periods of likely conflict can be pinpointed with ease. The following illustrative list is adapted from Dr. Samuel R. Chand's *Futuring*.

PREDICTABLE TIMES OF CONFLICT IN CHURCHES:

- Special days such as Christmas and Easter
- Special occasions such as weddings, funerals, and celebrations
- Occasions of fund-raising and budgeting
- The arrival of new staff
- Changes in leadership style whether in new or ongoing leadership
- The absence of the pastor on vacation, study-time or sick leave
- Changes in the family of the pastor, including marriage, divorce, birth, and death
- Rising leadership of new generations

Whether or not conflict is predictable or healthy, times of conflict take a toll on the church and its leadership. On one hand, shell-shocked pastors came for guidance because constant battles hampered the practice of ministry. On the other hand, disturbed and unsettled church leaders called upon our department for advice, guidance, and comfort in their efforts to become useful partners in ministry. The responsibility for these tumultuous disagreements sometimes lay with the minister, sometimes with lay leaders, and occasionally the blame fell on both sides.

> CONFLICT AMONG THE PEOPLE OF GOD IS AS OLD AS CAIN AND ABEL.

Sadly, I have often encountered lay leaders and ministers who merely glory in a title without seriously committing themselves to the mission and ministry of Jesus Christ. During my service on the Department of Black Church Relations, church members complained to me that their pastors were dictators. For their part, pastors bitterly charged that their members resisted all efforts to lead them

Chapter Two • *The Roots of the Problem*

toward change and growth.

The level of conflict in some congregations is shocking. I've heard of a South Carolina church whose ruling board fought so bitterly that the congregation felt it unseemly to allow such violent arguments within the church building. So a separate building was raised on a far corner of the property for the exclusive use of the cantankerous board.

Worse yet, a few years ago in a congregation in Maine, a member of the church added arsenic to the coffee at a church board meeting. Two people died from the poisoning. The poisoner's motive? A Communion table donated by his family wasn't being used regularly. Conflict among the people of God is as old as Cain and Abel.

HISTORICAL MARKERS

Within the black church, the causes of disagreement spring from conditions inherent in the experience of black Christians in this country. Through my experiences with troubled churches, I became convinced that the roots of church conflict within black

> OPPORTUNITIES FOR BLACK LEADERSHIP ARE SO LIMITED...

congregations could usually be traced to two sources: the presence of cultural patterns unique to the black church and the absence of vision-driven programs and planning.

Within the predominant culture of our country, the majority of blacks have been drained of self-worth and individual promise. Substandard wages, minimal expectations, and qustionable morals are conditions and/or myths laid upon blacks by the prevailing culture.

In reaction against social oppression, the black church provides a counter-cultural community wherein the people gather to experience the truth of their lives as lived together in the struggle for freedom. Today, as in the past, many blacks can lay their unconditional claim on no other institution except the church.

The Sunday morning worship service in a black church is still a gathering place for persons who possess little worth in the eyes of the dominant culture. In the typical black congregation one finds a disproportionate number of maids, janitors, and common laborers. Even those who have successfully climbed the professional, managerial ladder may feel that their accomplishments are tainted by the stigma of affirmative action.

These people, demeaned and belittled by the outside world, have the opportunity to become leaders and influencers within the church. In some churches, senior female members are recognized as "head mothers." Both men and women become highly respected deacons. Others aspire to leadership roles ranging from the president of the church auxiliary to the choir conductor. Black Christians who so often accept subservient roles during the week may explore their gifts and talents on Sunday in a supportive and loving community.

> CHRISTIANS CAN CELEBRATE THE INDIVIDUAL WORTH OF EACH PERSON

We can readily understand why some black Christians succumb to turf protection and competition for power. Opportunities for black leadership are so limited in America that the congregation sometimes becomes a battleground for those who have been denied access to power in every other venue of life.

Pastors are not necessarily above these power struggles. The black minister has a historical role of such authority and prestige that some pastors are tempted to function as dictators. The strong-man pastor whose every word is law provides the traditional model in many churches, but the faithful and effective minister will be guided more by love for the people than by love for power. The good pastor struggles to lead by assisting members to own a vision of the church

Chapter Two • *The Roots of the Problem*

and to grow into their calling to be kingdom builders.

Many unhealthy habits are deeply engrained in the black church. Boards of deacons and trustees will continue to hold the reins in some churches, and in other churches despotic pastors will ride roughshod over their members. Although planned change will occur only slowly, congregational worship offers a forum to explore new forms of partnership. The black church emphasizes the importance of the preacher and the centrality of the sermon. Ideally, the people of God will participate fully in Sunday morning worship. In the context of worship, the contribution and conduct of each member matters. Together the family of faith forms a clear understanding of God's calling, purpose, and the significant need for all members in the body of Christ to be involved in ministry.

The black church is in a unique position to recognize and affirm the value of every member, both the subdued and vocal. Within the body of Christ, black Christians can celebrate the individual worth of each person while creating a community of shared goals and a common mind. This dual commitment to individuality and community has both spiritual and social ramifications. Thus, a part of the kingdom of God is actualized or made visible.

The church is a community of believers who can freely share power and authority while appreciating the work of all human beings. This raises an intriguing challenge. Within the church, all who profess Christ are equipped and encouraged to share their individual gifts for the edification of the whole.

MISSION AND CALLING OF THE BLACK CHURCH

The black church in America emerged from white Christianity's distortion of the gospel message. The practice of slavery, particularly in the 18th and 19th centuries, offered Christianity to a disenfranchised people but refused full participation in white churches. The experience of a Virginia-born slave named George Liele is instructive. After his emancipation, Liele traveled up and down the Savannah River in Georgia, preaching to slaves wherever friendly plantation owners permitted. He founded several churches, but eventually Liele fled to Jamaica in 1783 because he was afraid of being forced back into slavery.

Liele's precarious freedom, his reliance upon the permission of white plantation owners, and the segregated black worship services shaped the unique character of the black church. Meanwhile, the white church was silent for the most part or even provided theological legitimization for slave codes and subsequent Jim Crow segregation laws.

The origins of the black church clearly define its nature and calling. Black Christianity is an oppressed people formed by the creative power of God in the liberating work of Jesus Christ and the empowering of the Holy Spirit. This liberated community of faith participates in divine actions to create God's kingdom of free humanity in the world. The black church embodies this theme of liberation by naming oppression and articulating hope through songs, stories, literature, lamentation, celebration, and preaching.

A THEOLOGY OF LIBERATION

The Bible is the starting point in developing a theology of liberation. Holy Scripture reveals that God elected the Israelites while they were oppressed in Egypt. This gracious choosing of an enslaved people provides the grounding for our understanding of God as the divine liberator who enters into human struggles for freedom.

Consider how the theophany at Sinai illuminates the politics of God:

"And Moses went up to God, and the LORD called to him from

the mountain, saying, 'Thus you shall say to the house of Jacob, and tell the children of Israel: "You have seen what I did to the Egyptians, and how I bore you on eagles' wings and brought you to Myself. Now therefore, if you will indeed obey My voice and keep My covenant, then you shall be a special treasure to Me above all people; for all the earth is Mine. And you shall be to Me a kingdom of priests and a holy nation." These are the words which you shall speak to the children of Israel.'" (Exodus 19:3-6)

This God identifies with an oppressed community of faith and reaffirms his earlier covenant with Abraham:

'I will make you exceedingly fruitful; and I will make nations of you, and kings shall come from you. And I will establish My covenant between Me and you and your descendants after you in their generations, for an everlasting covenant, to be God to you and your descendants after you. Also I give to you and your descendants after you the land in which you are a stranger, all the land of Canaan, as an everlasting possession; and I will be their God." (Genesis 17:6-8)

True to the promise, God eventually graces them with a land of their own.

Israel's experience of pain and hope in the struggle for liberation is further amplified in Old Testament prophecy that reveals Yahweh's concern for justice within the chosen community as an example to all nations. The 8th Century BC prophet Amos echoed this theme in his preaching when he thundered,

"But let justice run down like water, and righteousness like a mighty stream." (Amos 5:24).

Thus, the Old Testament story discloses Yahweh as the God of the oppressed who participates in the struggle for freedom and human dignity.

Jesus reaffirmed the theme of liberation when he grounded his ministry in the prophetic tradition. In his "inaugural sermon" Jesus offered himself as the fulfillment of the prophet Isaiah's vision of the jubilee—the year of release from bondage and debt.

"The Spirit of the LORD is upon Me, because He has anointed Me to preach the gospel to the poor; He has sent Me to heal the brokenhearted, to proclaim liberty to the captives and recovery of sight to the blind, to set at liberty those who are oppressed; to proclaim the acceptable year of the LORD." (Luke 4:18, 19).

The black church receives its mission, calling, and identity from these scriptural themes. The Bible, therefore, articulates the faith of two oppressed faith communities—Israel and the New Testament Church—whose freedom is inextricably bound to the divine economy operative in human liberation as fully disclosed in Jesus Christ.

THE BLACK PASTOR

In a church whose life grows from the gospel of liberation, what is the role of the pastor? My perceptions reflect my personal experience of the black minister and the black church. In my Christian and social community, as well as in most black communities, the ministerial profession was the first and almost only one to gain a foothold in the community. Not only does the pastor's role have historical precedence and prominence, but it also enjoys divine sanction.

> ...THE MISSION OF THE CHURCH IS TO INVOLVE THE UNINVOLVED.

These factors combine to make the preacher/minister supreme among black leaders. The noted black scholar, W. E. B. DuBois, wrote in The Souls of Black Folk:

> The black preacher is the most unique personality developed by blacks on American soil. He is a leader, a politician, an orator, a "boss", an intriguer, an idealist—all these qualities the black clergy possesses.

Chapter Two • *The Roots of the Problem*

Throughout my ministerial journey, I have struggled to fit into the role designated for the black minister. This has often created an inner conflict between my theology and the expectations of black church tradition. When I lived up to DuBois' description of "the boss", I preached and ran "my" church with no partnering and an iron hand. While I ran the show, I couldn't awaken any sense of service among church members. Although my individual efforts maintained peace and loyalty among the parish members and the surrounding community, the congregation had no spirit of joint ministry and cooperation.

My discontent with this situation drove me to explore other ways to function as a church leader. As I mature biblically, theologically, and spiritually, I struggle to remember that the church belongs not to me, but to Christ. The Head of the church intends for clergy and laity to work in partnership to fulfill the mission and life of the body of Christ.

Ephesians 4 teaches that God calls the pastor to equip the saints, not boss them. Nor can the pastor or a handful of key church leaders accomplish the whole work of the church. Therefore, the mission of the church is to involve the uninvolved. With this revolutionary shift in mind, leadership demands a new focus in most black churches. Pastoral efforts to win approval and support for church programming by doing everything single-handedly will ultimately lead to defeat.

The Iditarod dogsled race is one of the most grueling and demanding challenges in the world. A team of dogs pulls a heavy sled over rugged terrain in terrible weather, struggling for days to be the first across the finish line. In an interview with an Iditarod winner, the reporter asked the secret of the dogsled driver's success. The driver shrugged and said, "I train each of my dogs to be a leader." That sums up my vision of the black church's mission, empowering every member to pull together and share leadership while running the race set before us.

PARTNERSHIP AND LEADERSHIP

Leadership style is very strong and extremely important in the black Baptist Church. (Again I will speak out of my own tradition, but I believe my ideas apply to black churches in general.) The leader is highly respected, even revered, as is the judge presiding over the courtroom. This traditional emphasis on strong leadership began in the aftermath of the Civil War. In that postslavery culture, most impoverished black churches worshiped irregularly. The part-time pastor came to the church only once or twice in a month of Sundays. As a direct result of this sporadic pastoral presence and the absence of hands-on leadership, the church enjoyed very few long-term programs of ministry.

> MODERN PASTORS HAVE DEVELOPED EXPERTISE AS LEADERS...

In the void left by itinerant pastors, lay leaders rose to guide and strengthen the church. The deacons or a group of hand picked leaders assumed most of the care and nurture of the church when the pastor was absent—and the pastor was usually absent. The pastor was required to preach, conduct funerals and weddings, but lay leaders presided over the rest of congregational life. These voluntary leaders might even dictate the length and subject matter of the minister's sermons. The power of the deacons became concentrated, stable, and unchanging.

Unfortunately, many black churches in our nation still operate in this manner. As I have already pointed out, this pattern reflects the historical culture of the black church. The pattern is perpetuated by a regrettable lack of vision and the congregational programming that emerges from a shared vision. Black churches cling to the old way of doing things even though those habits no longer serve us well.

At the other extreme, some congregations expect the pastor to be responsible for everything. Nowadays the church is blessed with a growing number of trained clergy who devote full-time service to the local church. Modern pastors have developed expertise as leaders, executives, and administrators. As the pendulum swings the other way, too many congregations hold the pastor responsible for the totality of life and work in the church.

In a course on *The Theory of Organizational Behavior*, Robert Worley helped me see the end result of this trend. Eventually pastors become marketers of religion, driven by church expectations to maintain worship attendance, bring in new members, and cultivate congregational fellowship and spirituality.

Although these expectations invite the pastor to become a dictatorial manager, the contemporary black minister must undertake just the opposite. The black church needs ministers who will refuse to carry the whole workload of the church and will focus their efforts on building up the body of Christ both individually and collectively. The effective pastor gathers a people, reminding them of their calling, equipping them for mission, and sending them out to serve in the name of Christ.

> EACH CHRISTIAN HAS A PLACE IN THE HOUSEHOLD OF GOD…

The black pastor faces the challenge to awaken every member to the call of Christ so that a true community may emerge, a community of shared goals and responsibility. In the body of Christ, the contributions of each member are both sought and welcomed. When a congregation becomes a genuine community, the church embodies God's concern for the self, the neighborhood, and even the world. Of course, this approach to ministry requires members to think and act in new ways.

LESSONS IN LEADERSHIP

Jewish philosopher and theologian Martin Buber draws on biblical models to offer relevant lessons about leadership. Buber asserts that God often inverts the values of the world, choosing the weak and humble to lead. For instance, note the recurring choice of the younger son as the bearer of covenant responsibility. Abel, Jacob, Joseph, Moses, and David illustrate this preference for the younger, less privileged offspring.

Buber further underlines God's unexpected approach to leadership by recalling that God's purpose is fulfilled neither by might nor by power, but "by my Spirit," (Zechariah 4:6). Biblical leaders, Buber concludes, are leaders only in so far as they are themselves led by the Spirit of God.

The Old Testament figure of Moses exemplifies Buber's thinking and also represents a powerful role model within black Christianity. Like Moses, the faithful leader guides the wandering people of God through the wilderness of temptation and distraction. Without this crucial leadership, there would be no people as such. From this example we draw a valuable understanding. The pastoral leader forms and guides a people who are seeking and open to direction.

Like our judicial system, which is aimed at protecting basic rights, the black church traditionally served as an extended family for people whose own foundational core of family and security could be removed at a moment's notice. Avery Dulles refers to these ties of the Christian family as mystical Communion. Since congregational leaders are often viewed as spiritual parents, the church family grants all power to the pastor or deacons in the polity of the black Baptist Church. These leaders are not always male. For instance, elderly and spiritually mature women are often held up as role models on the so-called Mother's Board. Many churches have female clergy and some have empowered women as deacons.

A church structure of this sort leads to exclusiveness, bestowing special privileges upon an elite class of church members. The black church must strive to make all members feel fully affiliated with the church family. Each Christian has a place in the household of God and the right to provide input in the total life of the church. In this way, the believer fulfills the need to identify with the family of Christ gathered for worship on Sunday and scattered for service through the week.

This brief historical survey, by no means unique to the Baptist Church, helps frame the task before us: the full and vital inclusion of God's children who feel disinherited from the culture at large.

3

CONFRONTING THE PROBLEM

RECLAIMING LOST STORIES

In a 1965 interview with *Ebony* magazine, Dr. Martin Luther King, Jr. said that we blacks have to confront the fact that the Negro has not developed a sense of stewardship. Slavery was so divisive and brutal, so purposely molded to break the ties of community, that we never developed a sense of oneness. Even the family unit, the most basic building block of society, was undermined by slavery. The pattern of disunity that Negroes experience today derives from this cruel fact of history.

One of the sad effects of this social disintegration is the loss of history. Rightly understood, history is the story of a people, and if persons do not recognize themselves as belonging to a unified people, their story is fragmented or lost. This definitely affects the recording and keeping of church history.

Why is history important? Without a clear, compelling story, we don't understand our identity or purpose. Lacking a clearly defined identity, we have no guidelines to mold our behavior and no mission to claim our loyalty. Many of the problems evident in black churches today derive from lost or distorted history.

No wonder the antebellum slave owners worked so hard to squash and belittle the folktales that circulated among blacks. According to scholars, those folktales preserved the heritage left behind in Africa, as evidenced by the significant number of slave stories about animals such as lions, elephants, and monkeys. The lively retelling and adapting of those stories gave slaves a sense of culture and history. To this day the importance of story-telling and oral communication survives in the vitality of black preaching.

Prosecutors and defense lawyers learn to weave a convincing story, a powerful skill to master. The art of story telling conveys the message and persuades the jury or judge. Similarly, the art of story telling remains extremely important in the black church. From the "amen corner" listeners encourage the preacher, exclaiming, "Tell the story!"

> LACKING A CLEARLY DEFINED IDENTITY...

In *Models of the Church*, Avery Dulles maintains that this is an example of the church as herald. We live by stories that have been handed down to us. These stories often become vision-shaping symbols, clarifying or distorting our notions about God and the church. When these stories are lost or forgotten, the church is diminished. Reclaiming a healthy vision of the church means maintaining our stories, preserving our collective history. This means honoring the stories contributed by each person and finding a way to make sure those stories are passed along, preferably in written form.

Chapter Three • *Confronting the Problem*

FREEDOM AND POWER

As stated earlier, in the black church the development and performance of ministry has largely been the sole task of the pastor or has been delegated to a small group of leaders such as the Deacons or a Board of Directors. Sometimes the sharing of power is offered minimally to a few members of the congregation. When we explore our story, we see how this pattern originated from the poverty and oppression inherited from slavery.

But if God's people are called from bondage and oppression into a place of freedom, then the church is called to be free and to set at liberty those who are oppressed. The "priesthood of all believers" provides a model for partnership and mutuality allowing the black church to reclaim a significant aspect of the New Testament story, a part of the Christian story that offers healing from the devastating story of slavery.

In practice, this means a willingness to share power and conduct ministry in non-coercive ways. If black Christians truly believe in the "priesthood of all believers," the planning and performance of ministry—and even the writing of church history—will be tasks shared by clergy and laity alike. No longer will an individual or a select few determine the mission and ministry of the congregation. By its very nature, the church is a people called of God, a community called to partnership in ministry. Direction, decisions, and the work of ministry are the task of the entire church.

> GOD'S PEOPLE ARE CALLED FROM BONDAGE

LIVING UNDER GOD'S JURISDICTION

To return to the idea of the courtroom, my service on jury duty informs my thinking on the subject. A pool of jurors gathers at the stated time and each person is on call. Some might serve today, some next week, some are dismissed, but everyone is expected to report for duty.

Those who fail to honor their commitment answer to the judge. Once a particular jury panel is chosen, each person listens, ponders, questions and expresses an opinion. In the jury room, no person is discounted. Each voice counts. The jury foreman creates an orderly process so that every person has the opportunity to participate. Together, through a process of sharing, persuasion, and compromise, the diverse members of the jury complete a single task and bring a unified verdict.

> PRIMARY OBJECTIVES OF THE CHURCH...

I pray for the day that church members will work together with as much devotion and single-minded purpose as the typical jury. One of the primary objectives of the church is to help members belong to the whole work of the congregation. This vision requires participatory ministry, utilizing the full range of gifts given to all members. Church history—the collective story of all members—will thrive. Leadership will expand beyond the minister and deacons until the church becomes the true body of Christ led by the people of God.

SUNDAY SLOBS

We can see clearly how far we are from genuinely shared responsibility in the church when we observe the irresponsible behavior of some members. For example, some worshipers habitually stop at one of the local fast food restaurants on their way to church.

Chapter Three • *Confronting the Problem*

They bring greasy bags containing sausage biscuits, French fries, and cherry tarts into the sanctuary. Lacking the discipline to get their children out of bed early enough to feed and groom them before worship, some parents prefer to feed Junior during the service as if the sanctuary were a cafeteria. For months on end, we are forced to place in our Sunday bulletin a request for worshipers to refrain from eating in the sanctuary.

Not only are the parents undisciplined, so are the children. Food and refreshments doled out during worship serve as bribes to keep Junior quiet. Modern parenting techniques have replaced many former rules for raising children. I don't condone unnecessary harshness with youngsters, but perhaps we have gone too far in "sparing the rod." When I attended church as a child, misbehavior prompted immediate discipline—and not always from my own parents. Our congregation functioned as an extended family and any nearby adult might intervene to correct juvenile antics. If that adult then mentioned the incident to my parents, I could expect a second dose of correction when we arrived at home.

> RESPECT FOR THE LORD'S HOUSE IS AT LOW EBB.

If Sunday morning worship is not immune from carry-in feasting, neither is any other gathering of Christ's people. Members slurp soft drinks and munch on chips, cookies, and candies at choir rehearsal, at prayer services, and at meetings of every variety. To accompany the snacking, beeping pagers interrupt the flow of worship. Cell phone conversations take precedence over attention to the worship of God.

At the very least one would expect the trash from pew picnics to be deposited in the nearest wastebasket. But these folks lack the common decency to clean up after themselves. Instead, wrappers, cups and leaking catsup packets are left scattered in the pew. Apparently clean-up is the responsibility of the church janitor, not the people who made the mess.

In a spirit of honest confession, let me admit that my own behavior as a boy was not always impeccable. Sometimes my friends and I withheld some of our Sunday School offering, sneaked out of church, and visited a nearby store to satisfy a sweet tooth. To our credit, we did have the decency and respect to eat our purchases before we came back into church!

CLEANING UP OUR ACT

My oldest brother is a pastor in Tennessee. He and his son also operate an upholstery business on the side. Recently, they received a contract to re-cover the pews of a church in their city. In the process of the job, he and his son retrieved from the underside of the old pews a large bucket of chewing gum wads. From the creases and crevices of the old covers, they found discarded trash, including food crumbs and the remnants of piecrusts. Can you imagine the results of sitting on this trash while wearing a fine suit or a silk dress?

> MEMBERS MUST LEARN THE CRITICAL IMPORTANCE OF DECORUM AND DIGNITY.

Nor is that church unique. The janitor at our church once found a lottery ticket and a cocaine wrapper in the hymnal rack. Respect for the Lord's house is at low ebb. We must challenge and reverse this trend. During the welcome period in the church, we often invite visitors and members to sit back and relax. I contend we cannot afford to relax while disrespect for God's house is growing. This trend will never reverse unless we enter the struggle to correct this breakdown in structure.

While vacationing, my family and I have toured magnificently structured cathedrals. When we visited some of the great church buildings and cathedrals, the conduct of the tour guides made an impression on me. Our leaders spoke quietly and respectfully so that our presence might not interrupt those who had come to light candles and pray. I envied the reverence evident in those ancient churches.

One might expect tourists to behave crassly while touring someone else's church, but quite the opposite is true. In every place we visited, signs clearly designated certain areas "off limits." Visitors and sightseers honored those limits and respected those boundaries. How remarkable to observe strangers showing more reverence for the church than its own members.

BORED BELIEVERS?

We need only turn on the television to note the contrast between respectful tourists and the indifferent behavior of our own worshipers. Many churches now televise their services, providing a valuable ministry of broadcast and outreach. Unfortunately, these public services present a spectacle of disturbing and ill-mannered behavior. The camera's unblinking eye reveals people talking and chewing gum. Choir members, in plain view of the camera, stare vacantly into space or take part in animated conversations. People and leaders alike sit in pews looking bored or even sleeping.

During a recent cable televised worship service, I observed a person seated behind the pulpit area yawning and stretching as if he had just awakened from a restful night's sleep. Why does the church allow behavior that would arouse the judge's wrath in a court of law? Our members must learn the critical importance of decorum and dignity. Does the courtroom judge deserve greater deference than the Judge of all flesh? When contemporary worship emphasizes entertainment over introspection, we have shifted the focus from God to ourselves.

The contemporary church would be so much stronger and vibrant if we could recapture the Biblical zeal for worship.
- Noah worshiped God when the flood ended.
- Moses worshiped God on the mountain.
- David worshiped God when the Ark returned to the temple.
- The wise men worshiped God at the finding of Jesus.
- Mary and Joseph worshiped God when they dedicated Jesus.
- The blind man worshiped God when he received his sight.
- Mary worshiped God at the tomb on resurrection morning.
- The 120 worshiped God in the Upper Room and the Holy Ghost fell upon them.
- Peter worshiped God and preached by the seaside.
- Paul and Silas worshiped God in a jail cell.
- John worshiped God on the Isle of Patmos and was given a revelation.

Devoted and faithful worship transforms the church and uplifts the holiness and greatness of God. Most of the tasks that occupy the earthly church will be left behind when we got to heaven. No more ministering to the sick and heartbroken in heaven. No more assisting the poor. No more repentance. No more evangelizing. But worship will continue in heaven. Worship is the everlasting calling of the church.

When we worship God—
- The Father will be glorified!
- The Son will be magnified!
- The Spirit will be gratified!
- The Bible will be ratified!
- The Church will be edified!
- The Soul will be satisfied!
- The Devil will be horrified!

Chapter Three • *Confronting the Problem*

ON TIME AND ON BOARD

My wife made a keen observation during a summer travel tour. When the hotel personnel instructed us to be at the departure site for a Holy Land cruise at a certain time, all who paid their fares were present. The schedule was tight and the leader allowed no leeway for those who ran late. No one broke the rules or procedures. All the travelers were cooperative even though they had paid their money for the tour. No one expressed the attitude sadly common in today's church: "I paid my money and I can do anything I want."

At the Pearl Harbor Memorial, we shuttled to the area in a small boat. The official from the Navy said, "While traveling to the USS Arizona Memorial site, you are welcome to take pictures but remain seated." That made sense, but then the officer pressed his point home. "You are under the jurisdiction of the United States Navy, and we will ask you to leave the boat if any Navy guidelines are violated."

> CHURCHES HAVE BECOME FEARFUL OF EXPECTING—MUCH LESS DEMANDING

No one on the shuttle balked or objected, although most were U.S. citizens and therefore taxpayers. Furthermore, all of us had paid our entrance, transportation, and tour fees. No one protested because we knew that if we did not follow the rules, we would be put off the boat.

My heart sank when I compared the attitude on that shuttle to the prevailing attitude in the church. If a minister made a similar statement to church members and visitors during a worship service, that request would awaken angry protests and threats to attend another church. Churches have become fearful of expecting—much less demanding—reasonable standards of behavior. Pastors worry that they will lose popularity and support if they address these issues.

Nevertheless, a clear and consistent statement of essential standards would alleviate any of the problems we have cited so far. We would see an immediate renewal of respect for the house of God if church leaders united to enforce a common mandate: While a person is in and under the jurisdiction of the church, misbehavior will not be tolerated.

MENTORS AND ROLE MODELS

As mentioned earlier, the leadership of the church must accept serious responsibility for congregational behavior. The pastor, officers, auxiliary, and ministry leaders are role models for proper church behavior. We must believe and lift up to the people, "Follow me as I follow Christ." By personal example, we must teach the value of order in the church. While never ignoring the liberating presence of God's Spirit, we must also maintain acceptable decorum.

God exhibited divinely ordained order when creating the world. God did not create the animals before there was light to guide their feet. The fish of the sea did not precede the waters of the deep. God did not give life to flying things until there was a sky in which they could spread their wings. Some supposedly spiritual folk criticize churches that have an order of worship. However, the order of worship is a guide for God's people, not a yoke of bondage. We must always allow the Holy Spirit to alter and modify our worship, but decency and order are the hallmarks of the Spirit's presence.

> WHILE NEVER IGNORING THE LIBERATING PRESENCE OF GOD'S SPIRIT, WE MUST ALSO MAINTAIN ACCEPTABLE DECORUM.

One reason for the decline in church etiquette in recent years is the loss of training union programs. The names and terminology may differ between denominations, but in years past most churches offered a weekly training program, typically on Sunday afternoon or evening. The Methodist Church, Church of God in Christ, and the Catholic Church had fellowships or unions dedicated to teaching church behavior, doctrine, procedure, order, and etiquette. My own tradition had the Baptist Training Union (BTU), originally called the Baptist Young Peoples Union (BYPU).

The BTU provided a training ground for youngsters, active church members, and adult leaders. In the weekly gatherings of the Baptist Training Union, I learned lessons that have served me ever since: how to pray, how to properly read Scripture, when it was proper to walk in and out of the church worship service, and how to address the pulpit when giving a welcome address or making public remarks. In short, we learned how to behave in church. Training union was a safe place for honestly and openly addressing problems and hard questions.

I offer this guide to the church at large in the hope that this volume will serve as a training union on paper. You may wish to make this book available to members of your church, or you may use the material here as a guide for your own training sessions and lesson plans. I do not want to dwell on the theoretical, but prefer to draft a practical handbook.

> GOD EXHIBITED DIVINELY ORDAINED ORDER WHEN CREATING THE WORLD.

To this end, I present the following list to summarize and encapsulate much of the desirable behavior we strive for in the church.

I do not name these the Twelve Commandments. These are not written in stone, but God has impressed them upon my heart. I believe they will give helpful guidance to all God's people.

TWELVE POINTS TO PONDER AND PRACTICE

Point One: Be on time.

You need at least five minutes after your arrival at the church building to prepare for worship. View every visit to the church, even to attend a committee meeting, as an opportunity for worship. Arrive early to compose your body and mind to be sensitive to the Holy Spirit and to whisper a prayer before the service begins.

A fellow pastor told me about a bride who arrived twenty minutes late for her own wedding. The day was warm and the sanctuary windows were open, so every head turned when the bride's car screeched to a halt outside the door. The bride emerged from the car with dress disheveled, carrying her shoes and struggling to balance flowers, veil, and cosmetic kit. Seeing the worshipers staring at her from within the church, she shouted through the window, "I could use a little help out here!"

> ...DECENCY AND ORDER ARE THE HALLMARKS OF THE SPIRIT'S PRESENCE.

I don't know what caused her tardiness, but I'm quite sure she was not in a worshipful spirit when she came down the aisle. On a lesser scale, a similar scene plays out every Sunday morning as folks rush in at the last minute—or several minutes after the last minute—because they slept in or lingered too long over coffee and the morning newspaper.

Good worship requires good preparation. That preparation should begin on Saturday with the habit of laying out our church clothes and offering before going to bed. Those who have shopped to exhaustion on Saturday or stayed up too late or partied into the wee hours are ill-prepared to approach God in a solemn and focused spirit. Rather than rushing into worship breathless and flustered, allow a few minutes to settle the body and focus the heart before entering into the presence of the Almighty.

> ARRIVE EARLY...

My elders taught me to take care of personal needs and conduct church business matters before entering the sanctuary for worship. Apparently some worshipers labor under the impression that the bathroom facilities remain closed most of the time, only opening when the organist begins the prelude.

Parents, teach your children that that there are appropriate times in church for recesses and breaks. Your children are already accustomed to this discipline during the school day. Teachers do not allow students to get up during the class period and excuse themselves, nor should we encourage our youngsters to wander in and out of the sanctuary on a whim.

Adults should take the same lesson to heart. Sometimes the pressures of medication offer an excuse for leaving during the service, but I know that many who avail themselves of this pretense haven't been to a doctor in years.

When my members are honest with me, they admit to leaving the service for trivial reasons: a stretch break, a bit of socializing, or responding to pagers or cell phones. Unless a member is on call at the hospital or expecting a call from the president, beepers and phones should be turned off so one's full attention can be given to God. Following the rules of yesteryear would end most of this aimless wandering. Attend to all personal needs before the worship begins.

> GOOD WORSHIP REQUIRES GOOD PREPARATION.

One must arrive at the House of God on time. Better yet, come early. Too many of our churches publicize and advertise that worship begins at 11:00 a.m., and yet we consistently start late due to sloppy leadership or because we are waiting for a sufficient number of people to arrive. I do not advocate becoming a slave to the clock, but we must respect timeliness. If people cannot rely on us to begin the service on time, how can they trust us to impart the truths of eternity?

> ATTEND TO ALL PERSONAL NEEDS BEFORE THE WORSHIP BEGINS.

Point Two:
Never pass up the aisle during prayer or Scripture reading.

If you must be excused, your presence and movement will distract and draw attention away from the pulpit. Therefore, take great pains to leave as quietly as possible.

During the invitational period, avoid unnecessary walking. This is an eternal time. Souls hang in the balance of salvation and damnation. Be very sensitive to the moving of the Holy Spirit during this time of worship. Your praying is essential; your strolling is not.

As a general rule, we can establish several points in the service when worshipers should never walk about or excuse themselves:
- during the Invitation to Discipleship;
- during the reading of the Scripture;
- during prayers for any occasions;
- during Baptism or the Lord's Supper; and
- during the preaching of the word of God.

When the bailiff calls out, **"All rise!"** everyone in the courtroom stands in respectful stillness, honoring the judge's entrance. Similarly, while the church is at prayer, all walking and movement must cease. In prayer we invite God to enter our worship and our hearts. Surely the Lord deserves our reverent stillness.

Just as a bailiff controls the entrances and exits of a courtroom,

Chapter Three • *Confronting the Problem*

an usher should close doors and turn toward the pulpit area to also join in the period of prayer. Within a service of worship, one prayer is no more important than another. One person may have the reputation of "praying heaven down" while another habitually raises a less lofty petition. Nevertheless, we must not show more respect for the former than the latter. For instance, many of us disregard the offertory prayer while giving whole-hearted attention to an altar prayer. In both cases, the same God waits to hear our prayer. Whether a court is convened to deal with a civil matter or a felony, we accord the presiding judge the same level of respect. Prayer is prayer regardless of placement in the service, subject matter, or who offers the prayer.

> "ALL RISE!"

We may learn an important lesson about worship in our own day by looking at the worship of Jesus' day.

"So He came to Nazareth, where He had been brought up. And as His custom was, He went into the synagogue on the Sabbath day, and stood up to read. And He was handed the book of the prophet Isaiah. And when He had opened the book, He found the place where it was written:

'The Spirit of the LORD is upon Me, because He has anointed Me to preach the gospel to the poor; He has sent Me to heal the brokenhearted, to proclaim liberty to the captives and recovery of sight to the blind, to set at liberty those who are oppressed; to proclaim the acceptable year of the LORD.'

Then He closed the book, and gave it back to the attendant and sat down. And the eyes of all who were in the synagogue were fixed on Him." (Luke 4:16-20)

When Jesus read in the synagogue from the book of Isaiah, the Bible states all eyes were fixed upon Him. Here is an excellent point of observation and comparison. When the Word of God is read, all eyes, all hearts, and all ears should be directed toward the reader of the Word. Some churches require worshipers to stand during the reading of Scripture. More and more people are bringing their Bibles to church and welcome the calling of their attention to the Word of God. Definitely, when Scripture is read, all other activity should stop.

When asked to participate in the worship service, you should stand, do what is requested, and then be seated. If you are asked to read the Scripture, you do not have to make opening remarks. If you bring a special announcement, do not preach a mini-sermon. If asked to pray, please do not make remarks or give a testimony. The words of welcome should not be a time of exhortation and personal agendas. In short, the worship service is neither a meeting of Toastmasters nor an improvisational comedy skit.

> SIMPLY DO THE TASK FOR WHICH YOU ARE CALLED ON.

I have requested people to pray during the offertory period and they become so wrapped up in their own ideas and thoughts that they utterly fail to mention the offering. Can you imagine a person praying grace over a meal and never mentioning the food? Simply do the task for which you are called on. Of course, the Holy Spirit can alter any assignment, but that is no license to ramble in word or thought. We often blame the Spirit when our real intent is "getting something off our chests." The attention you draw to yourself is attention drawn away from God.

To add to this point, when we extend the invitation for salvation and church membership, no one should be moving through the room except the ministers, church officers assisting in the invitation, and those coming forward in response. Any words or actions that divert attention from the invitational period may distract a soul in need. No one wants a sinner to bypass the invitation to accept Christ as Lord

Chapter Three • *Confronting the Problem*

and Savior due to inappropriate behavior during the most critical moment of worship. We must be serious about soul winning.

Do not use the invitation to Christian discipleship period to walk, talk, greet, or meet someone. Restrain your insistent bladder for a few more minutes. This is the most serious and meaningful part of the service. This may be the last time a man, woman, boy or girl will have a chance to accept Jesus as Lord and personal Savior. If you are not sure what to do or when to do it, ask an usher for guidance.

In the same vein, when the invitation period ends worshipers who make a mad dash for the exit doors dishonor the closing acts of worship. The end of worship is always the benediction, God's blessing upon the people for a productive week of Christian life and witness. Even if you spurn that blessing, do you dare allow your actions to rob someone else of that moment of peace and assurance?

Of course, remaining firmly planted in the pew throughout the service is no proof that one is giving full attention to the worship of God. Visitors have expressed to me their irritation and dismay at some pew behavior. Reading the church bulletin or newsletter while the choir is singing or a minister is speaking insults the leaders of the worship. Instead of fervently seeking God's face in worship, some members offer a running commentary on the service. Others converse with neighbors, write notes, ponder the hymnal, or leaf through Bible. These distracting behaviors build a wall between the worshiper and God.

Especially troubling to me is the habit of intentionally indulging in frivolous antics because of personal dislike or disrespect for the person who is speaking or performing. How can the body of Christ allow such spitefulness to interrupt our worship of God? Jesus counsels us to make things right with our brothers and sisters before entering God's presence. We would do well to take those words to heart.

- If any of you lacks wisdom, let him ask of God, who gives to all liberally and without reproach, and it will be given to him. But let him ask in faith, with no doubting, for he who doubts is like a wave of the sea driven and tossed by the wind. For let not that man suppose that he will receive any thing from the Lord; he is a double-minded man, unstable in all his ways. (James 1:5-8)
- Continue earnestly in prayer, being vigilant in it with thanksgiving; meanwhile praying also for us, that God would open to us a door for the word, to speak the mystery of Christ, for which I am also in chains, that I may make it manifest, as I ought to speak. Walk in wisdom toward those who are outside, redeeming the time. Let your speech always be with grace, seasoned with salt, that you may know how you ought to answer each one. (Colossians 4:2-6)
- But from there you will seek the LORD your God, and you will find Him if you seek Him with all your heart and with all your soul. When you are in distress, and all these things come upon you in the latter days, when you turn to the LORD your God and obey His voice (for the LORD your God is a merciful God), He will not forsake you nor destroy you, nor forget the covenant of your fathers which He swore to them. (Deuteronomy 4:29-31)

Point Three: Show respect for the worship service.

If the sermon has already begun, take a seat near the door as quietly and unobtrusively as possible. This applies even if you are in your home church and familiar with the seating arrangements. Ministers must never walk into the pulpit after the service has begun unless invited by the pastor to participate. Visiting deacons should be seated, as are all other worshipers. In most cases, deacons and ministers will be identified and invited by the persons in charge. Always be willing to participate in the service after being recognized, but do not put yourself forward. Choose a humble seat, and if you are to be exalted, let it be done by others.

Consider the teaching of our Lord in this matter.

"So He told a parable to those who were invited, when He noted how they chose the best places, saying to them: 'When you are invited by anyone to a wedding feast, do not sit down in the best place, lest one more honorable than you be invited by him; and he who invited you and him come and say to you, "Give place to this man," and then you begin with shame to take the lowest place. But when you are invited, go and sit down in the lowest place, so that when he who invited you comes he may say to you, "Friend, go up higher." Then you will have glory in the presence of those who sit at the table with you. For whoever exalts himself will be humbled, and he who humbles himself will be exalted.'" (Luke 14:7-11)

In many congregations ushers take a seat after the minister announces the text for the sermon. If your church has multiple services and other activities scheduled simultaneously with Sunday morning worship, you may wish to rethink this approach. Ushers assigned to the doors leading in and out of the sanctuary should remain on post at the door during the sermon. This insures that anyone entering worship during the sermon will be led to a specific seat.

If the worship service has begun and you arrive late, be seated as close to the door as possible or allow the ushers to lead you to whatever seat is readily available so that your entrance does not become a spectacle. Do not amble down the aisle looking for your special seat during worship.

On this same note, when a worshiper becomes ill or moves in any way during the sermon, all eyes and attention turn toward that individual. Such occasions will inevitably arise, and these concerns should be handled quickly, quietly, and without fanfare. Always minimize the embarrassment of the troubled person and the distraction to the rest of the congregation.

No minister should ever walk into the pulpit after the sermon has begun. Moreover, if you serve in the pulpit ministry, you should arrive at the church early. Our church is blessed with over forty licensed or ordained ministers, but we have fewer than ten seats in the pulpit. Each Sunday, some of the ministers must sit in the pews. We do ask, however, that a minister sit near the front whenever possible. At times during the year, deacons and ministers may sit and worship with their families, setting aside official duties on that day.

> PEW CONVERSATIONS DISAPPOINT VISITORS...

Point Four: Be devout in every attitude.

Studiously avoid all whispering. Share your hymnal and Bible with your neighbor. If you are visiting a church, always conform to its custom of worship.

When you find it necessary to speak a word to a neighbor or an usher, do so briefly and quietly. I have observed worshipers carrying on lengthy, detailed conversations. Some turn the entire body toward the person with whom they are talking. The ongoing conversation draws the attention of others, but glances and stares do not curb these chats. Rather the conversation simply grows more intense.

As a pastor, I sometimes wonder if I am too sensitive on this issue, blowing the matter out of proportion. However, videotaping worship services and choir concerts confirms the problem. Some adults are far more talkative than children during the service. Ministers and ushers find it awkward to address this issue while it is happening, but other members can make a difference. If someone insists on talking to you during the service, the best response is to say politely and firmly, "Excuse me, but we can continue this conversation after church." Pew conversations disappoint visitors, distract members, and express rudeness and disrespect toward the speakers and worship leaders.

I also encourage respect for the symbols of our faith and the furnishings that enhance and bless our worship. While visiting a church several months ago, I was appalled to witness a deacon making change and counting money on the Communion table. In bygone days, no one touched or moved the Communion table except for weddings or funerals. We honored—almost worshipped—the table reserved for the Lord's Supper. As children, we would not have shown disrespect for the table lest we draw down a lightning bolt of wrath. Perhaps we may have carried this too far, but a healthy reverence demands our respect for the visible signs of our faith and the furnishings that focus our attention upon God's presence.

> THE MINISTER SHOULD ALWAYS DISPLAY A SERVANT SPIRIT.

Point Five: Be thoughtful of the comfort of others.

Take the center of the pew from each side, if you are the first to enter. Leave all vacant space at the end next to the aisle for those who will need to be seated after your arrival. What a circus balancing act ensues when a latecomer must squeeze and totter between the feet and past the knees of those who refuse to surrender their aisle seats.

The leaders of the church must offer the first and foremost example of servanthood. Jesus has set the example. He came to serve, not to be served. The minister should always display a servant spirit. In its original meaning, the word "pastor" signified a shepherd.

What is the task of the shepherd if not to show love, nurture, and compassion for the sheep? The word "deacon" derives from the Greek word *diakonia* that means "table waiter." Although I have sometimes endured waiters who spent most of their time making phone calls and taking smoke breaks, the good waiter does not see to his/her own needs, but gives attention to those who are assigned to his care. Christ calls his leaders to serve the flock and wait on tables. Jesus was willing to wash the feet of others, and he expects similarly humble service from us.

As a culture, we have lost common courtesy for others. The bitter root of disrespect has grown up between men and women, young and old, and the "haves" and "have-nots." Shortly after moving to Atlanta, I found myself on a crowded city bus. People stood in the aisle while the bus rolled through the city. A well-intentioned gentleman offered his seat to a woman standing beside him. To my surprise, the woman loudly cursed the man, accusing him of degrading and demeaning her. Her voice carried through the whole bus as she took him to task for his humiliating and patronizing attitude.

> RESERVED SEATING SHOULD BE MINIMIZED.

"Do you think I'm too fragile to stand?" she shouted.

The woman's behavior shocked me, as well as most of my fellow bus riders. I am dismayed that the world has become so ungracious that simple courtesy evokes contempt.

Again allow me to address those who come into the worship service and stake claim to certain seats. Such behavior is not only inconsiderate, but also unchristian. Consider the message you communicate to brothers and sisters in Christ when you set anchor at the end of the pew and everyone else must crawl over you to be seated. I have seen church members actually glare at others who attempt to enter their "reserved" pew. Perhaps these pew-squatters believe they are fulfilling a biblical mandate, gluing their backsides to the pew as if to say, "I shall not be moved; like a tree planted, I shall not be moved."

An acquaintance who moved to a new city had an unfortunate experience while visiting a local church for the first time. My friend arrived a few minutes before the service and entered a large sanctuary that was nearly empty. He and his wife settled in an unoccupied pew near the rear. As soon as they seated themselves, a woman in the pew behind them said, "Those people sat right in front of us! Can you believe that? I can't see the pulpit now."

The woman and her companion could have slid a few feet in either direction in her empty pew, but she continued to complain loudly until my friend and his wife moved to a different spot. With such an attitude, perhaps you can guess why that cavernous sanctuary was almost empty. My friend and his wife never attended that church again.

If a coveted seat matters more than the love that ties us together in Christ, something is amiss in our faith. Reserved seating should be minimized. One cannot pretend to be the proprietor of a seat or pew. If one prefers a certain seat and the sanctuary fills quickly with worshipers, one needs to arrive early to insure the seat of preference.

If you know that you must leave the worship early or if you need to take medicine, do not sit in the first three rows of the church on Sunday morning or during worship service or ministry meetings. You will distract the congregation as you come and go. Instead, follow Jesus' advice to seek out a lowly seat—near the back!

- One thing I have desired of the LORD,
  That will I seek:
  That I may dwell in the house of the LORD
  All the days of my life,

- To behold the beauty of the LORD,
And to inquire in His temple. (Psalm 27:4)
- But the LORD is in His holy temple. Let all the earth keep silence before Him. (Habakkuk 2:20)
- Good and upright is the LORD;
Therefore He teaches sinners in the way.
The humble He guides in justice,
And the humble He teaches His way.
All the paths of the LORD are mercy and truth,
To such as keep His covenant and His testimonies.
For Your name's sake, O LORD,
Pardon my iniquity, for it is great. (Psalm 25:8-11)

Please do not draw attention by raising your hand and pointing your index fingers in the air as you excuse yourself. A poem from Kenneth Hugh Burton's *Bootleg CD's: Another Book of Poems* rightly pokes fun at this silly custom. I include the poem here with Mr. Burton's permission.

The Finger

I gave my church the finger one Sunday some years back
I was sitting there quite edgy with my listenin' not intact
I had heard that Bible story, I had heard it all before
I was sitting near the front but I was thinking 'bout the door
Now I do have me some manners and I'm not what you'd call rude
But my mind was now a racing and my thoughts were rather crude
So sitting there I remembered as I nodded, as I slept
That if the Lawd don't keep you, you just can't be kept
I waited for the right time when the preacher took a pause
before the second offering and said my final "thank you Lawds"
I raised my index finger, raised it just above my head
And excused myself from service and headed home to bed

Chapter Three • *Confronting the Problem*

Where did this practice begin in our churches? As a sister was leaving church one day, a little boy asked me, "Why is that lady telling us that she is number one?" Rather than drawing unnecessary attention, one should slip from the sanctuary as quietly and unobtrusively as possible.

I know the effort required of parents to bring their children to worship and I respect that commitment. Nonetheless, if your children misbehave or fuss during the service, please do not create an embarrassing spectacle by settling in the front pew. A seat near the rear will prevent others from being distracted during worship time. We gather in worship to seek a blessing. Parents—especially parents of energetic and rambunctious children—should make every effort to insure that their children do not undermine the worship experience for sisters and brothers in the Lord.

> ...DO NOT DRAW ATTENTION...

- Now this is the commandment, and these are the statutes and judgments which the LORD your God has commanded to teach you, that you may observe them in the land which you are crossing over to possess, that you may fear the LORD your God, to keep all His statutes and His commandments which I command you, you and your son and your grandson, all the days of your life, and that your days may be prolonged. Therefore hear, O Israel, and be careful to observe it, that it may be well with you, and that you may multiply greatly as the LORD God of your fathers has promised you—"a land flowing with milk and honey." Hear, O Israel: The LORD our God, the LORD is one! You shall love the LORD your God with all your heart, with all your soul, and with all your strength. And these words which I command you today shall be in your heart. You

shall teach them diligently to your children, and shall talk of them when you sit in your house, when you walk by the way, when you lie down, and when you rise up. You shall bind them as a sign on your hand, and they shall be as frontlets between your eyes. You shall write them on the doorposts of your house and on your gates.
(Deuteronomy 6:1-9)
- Train up a child in the way he should go, and when he is old he will not depart from it. (Proverbs 22:6)

Don't allow your children to cry for fifteen minutes during church services and activities before addressing the issue. Crying children are like good intentions: they should be carried out immediately. Effective church ushers will swiftly assist the parents of crying children.

- But the wisdom that is from above is first pure, then peaceable, gentle, willing to yield, full of mercy and good fruits, without partiality and without hypocrisy.
(James 3:17)
- That the God of our Lord Jesus Christ, the Father of glory, may give to you the spirit of wisdom and revelation in the knowledge of Him…(Ephesians 1:17)

Don't allow your children to tear up the pew Bible or draw funny faces in the hymnals in an attempt to pacify them during the Sunday morning service. These are the tools of our worship and should be treated with respect. If we do not model that respect for our children, how will they learn to approach God with reverence?

And whatever your age, if you must chew gum during church services, it would look much better in your mouth than plastered to the underside of the church pews.

- My son, do not forget my law,
  But let your heart keep my commands;

Chapter Three • *Confronting the Problem*

> For length of days and long life
> And peace they will add to you.
> Let not mercy and truth forsake you;
> Bind them around your neck,
> Write them on the tablet of your heart,
> And so find favor and high esteem
> In the sight of God and man.
> Trust in the LORD with all your heart,
> And lean not on your own understanding;
> In all your ways acknowledge Him,
> And He shall direct[a] your paths.
> My son, do not despise the chastening of the LORD,
> Nor detest His correction;
> For whom the LORD loves He corrects,
> Just as a father the son in whom he delights.
> (Proverbs 3:1-6, 11-12)

- He who spares his rod hates his son,
  But he who loves him disciplines him promptly.
  (Proverbs 13:24)

This same measure of respect pertains to the church building at large. Don't allow your children to run through the church as if it were a fast food restaurant play area. Both for their own safety and in courtesy to others, children should be closely supervised while in the church building or on the grounds. The church represents the House of God. A tender age is no excuse for dishonoring God's House. When God gives children to a couple, God also gives them responsibility for those children.

- Whom will he teach knowledge? And whom will he make
  to understand the message?
  Those just weaned from milk?
  Those just drawn from the breasts?

> For precept must be upon precept, precept upon precept, line upon line, line upon line, here a little, there a little. (Isaiah 28:9-10)
- All your children shall be taught by the LORD, and great shall be the peace of your children. (Isaiah 54:13)

Point Six: Be a welcoming committee of one.

While you should avoid drawing attention to yourself by indulging in conversation during worship, nevertheless strive to speak a bright, cheery word to as many as possible. Perhaps your church offers an opportunity for such greetings at a designated point during worship. If not, make time before or after the service for hearty and joyful fellowship.

Sincere friendliness is a drawing card to visitors. If you are sitting near visitors introduce them to the pastor or to some of the church leaders. Make certain you get their names and call them during the week to invite them back to your church. Many churches use visitor pew cards to register newcomers. Whatever method is preferred, prompt follow-up with visitors is crucial for the congregation that wishes to grow.

Nothing disheartens a church visitor more quickly than encountering sour, unfriendly people. We should check personal agendas, attitudes, and business concerns at the door when we arrive at church so we may focus our hearts on worship, preaching, and saving souls. Each and every member is the best—or worst—possible advertisement for the congregation. The pastor can preach with Spirit-filled power, the choir can sing until heaven falls, and the facilities may be immaculate and modern, but an unfriendly member will undo the best efforts with a single negative sentence.

Many visitors do not return for a second visit because they encounter an unkind spirit or attitude. Church folks sometimes act as if they are angry at God, angry at the pastor, angry at the church, and angry at life in general. If the real truth were told, they are angry at themselves. Faithful members should know better and do better. Treat each meeting with a visitor as if it were your only opportunity to make that person feel at home.

Point Seven: Properly address the pulpit and church body.

When a member comes before the church to address the body of Christ, order must prevail. Some make light of the manner in which the African-American church recognizes those seated in the pulpit and the honored leaders of the church. However, the older I become the more I am certain that we exalt God by practicing courtesy and decorum in the church. Suppose you opened your door to a visitor and that person simply walked into your home, sat where they pleased, and said nothing to acknowledge you. You would wonder if they lacked basic home training and courtesy. In effect, we fall into this same manner of rudeness when we disregard pastors and congregational leaders. Observe the following guidelines when standing before the church or a church gathering.

> GIVE PRIMARY REVERENCE AND HONOR TO GOD.

Give primary reverence and honor to God. Our Lord deserves first place in all things.

Then honor and recognize the pastor. Make sure to do this even if the pastor is not present. Recognizing the pastor's spouse is also appropriate. Typically, the pastor owes much of their success to the help and counsel of a spouse.

Tradition teaches us to recognize the Reverend Clergy. You may briefly note and recognize some of the clergy, ministers, or local dignitaries who have earned high honor and respect. Once we begin to call names and make special recognitions, we will probably offend some that feel they also deserve this honor and recognition. Be sensitive to those with tender feelings.

Recognize the official boards of the church, for they stand with the pastor in the health of the congregation and the success of the ministry.

Recognize the Mother's boards and other officials and leaders in the church.

Finally, recognize the brothers and sisters or members and visiting friends.

In the course of these greetings, polite and welcoming ministers and congregation members will answer the greetings with "Amen." Apathy and silence dampen the heartiest and most spirited greetings in the church. When someone says, "Good morning, church!" and receives no reply, the speaker feels defeated before beginning the second sentence. Whenever addressed, I always say thank you aloud for the person to hear and know I appreciate their respect and honor.

Some bitter souls argue that these respectful greetings smack of unhealthy admiration for men and women, but this courtesy has nothing to do with worshiping the creature over the Creator. I take liberty to return to the illustration that it is unchristian and unkind to come into someone's home without a show of respect for the head of the household.

Of course, particular customs differ from church to church and among various denominations. We may well allow leeway in the precise manner of showing respect when cultural differences come to bear. However, the underlying principle of honoring one another in Christ remains fundamental to church life.

Giving sincere honor to others encourages personal humility. Some of us would be better Christians, better choir members, ushers, trustees, presidents, or deacons if we lifted up the work of others and didn't chase after credit for our own efforts in the church.

- How lovely is Your tabernacle,
  O LORD of hosts!
  My soul longs, yes, even faints
  For the courts of the LORD;
  My heart and my flesh cry out for the living God.
  Even the sparrow has found a home,
  And the swallow a nest for herself,
  Where she may lay her young—
  Even Your altars, O LORD of hosts,
  My King and my God.
  Blessed are those who dwell in Your house;
  They will still be praising You. Selah
  Blessed is the man whose strength is in You,
  Whose heart is set on pilgrimage.
  As they pass through the Valley of Baca,
  They make it a spring;
  The rain also covers it with pools.
  They go from strength to strength;
  Each one appears before God in Zion.
  O LORD God of hosts, hear my prayer;
  Give ear, O God of Jacob! Selah
  O God, behold our shield,
  And look upon the face of Your anointed.
  For a day in Your courts is better than a thousand.
  I would rather be a doorkeeper in the house of my God
  Than dwell in the tents of wickedness.
  For the LORD God is a sun and shield;
  The LORD will give grace and glory;
  No good thing will He withhold
  From those who walk uprightly.
  O LORD of hosts,

Blessed is the man who trusts in You! (Psalm 84)
- Let your light so shine before men, that they may see your good works and glorify your Father in heaven. (Matthew 5:16)
- The wicked flee when no one pursues,
  But the righteous are bold as a lion.
  Because of the transgression of a land, many are its princes;
  But by a man of understanding and knowledge
  Right will be prolonged.
  A poor man who oppresses the poor
  Is like a driving rain which leaves no food.
  Those who forsake the law praise the wicked,
  But such as keep the law contend with them.
  Evil men do not understand justice,
  But those who seek the LORD understand all.
  He who covers his sins will not prosper,
  But whoever confesses and forsakes them will have mercy.
  (Proverbs 28:1-5,13)

Usher Ministries, Welcome Committees, choir loft, and pulpit are situations that call for kind and pleasant people. These ministries that make such an impression on visitors are no place for unsmiling sour-pusses with evil dispositions and ugly personalities.

- I beseech you therefore, brethren, by the mercies of God, that you present your bodies a living sacrifice, holy, acceptable to God, which is your reasonable service. And do not be conformed to this world, but be transformed by the renewing of your mind, that you may prove what is that good and acceptable and perfect will of God. For I say, through the grace given to me, to everyone who is among you, not to think of himself more highly than he ought to think, but to think soberly, as God has dealt to each one a measure of faith. For as we have many members in one body, but all the members do not have the same function, so we, being many, are one body in Christ, and individually members of one another. Having then gifts differing according to the grace that is given to us, let us use them: if prophecy, let us prophesy in proportion to our faith; or ministry, let us use it in our ministering; he who teaches, in teaching; he who exhorts, in exhortation; he who gives, with liberality; he who leads, with diligence; he who shows mercy, with cheerfulness. Let love be without hypocrisy. Abhor what is evil. Cling to what is good. Be kindly affectionate to one another with brotherly love, in honor giving preference to one another… (Romans 12:1-10)

- Beloved, let us love one another, for love is of God; and everyone who loves is born of God and knows God. He who does not love does not know God, for God is love. In this the love of God was manifested toward us, that God has sent His only begotten Son into the world, that we might live through Him. In this is love, not that we loved God, but that He loved us and sent His Son to be the propitiation for our sins. Beloved, if God so loved us, we also ought to love one another. (I John 4:7-11)

- Therefore, as the elect of God, holy and beloved, put on tender mercies, kindness, humility, meekness, longsuffering; bearing with one another, and forgiving one another, if anyone has a complaint against another; even as Christ forgave you, so you also must do. But above all these things put on love, which is the bond of perfection. And let the peace of God rule in your hearts, to which also you were called in one body; and be thankful. Let the word of Christ dwell in you richly in all wisdom, teaching and admonishing one another in psalms and hymns and spiritual songs, singing with grace in your hearts to the Lord. And whatever you do in word or deed, do all in the name of the Lord Jesus, giving thanks to God the Father through Him. (Colossians 3:12-17)

Point Eight: Depart from the church as reverently as you entered.

Never put on your coat or wrap during the closing hymn. Do not make a rush for the door immediately after the benediction is pronounced. Likewise, the church parking lot is a place to show Christian courtesy and patience. The religion of some people evaporates as soon as they turn the key in the ignition.

Show loving respect when the junior or youth ushers are on duty. This is no occasion to stroll in and out of the church. We should show special deference to young people assisting in the church and posted at the door. When the junior ushers are in uniform, they are in a position of authority. This authority stands, regardless of their age. If a person wants respect from others, he or she first must give it.

> IF A PERSON WANTS RESPECT FROM OTHERS, HE OR SHE FIRST MUST GIVE IT.

- Hear, O Israel: The LORD our God, the LORD is one! You shall love the LORD your God with all your heart, with all your soul, and with all your strength. And these words which I command you today shall be in your heart. You shall teach them diligently to your children, and shall talk of them when you sit in your house, when you walk by the way, when you lie down, and when you rise up. You shall bind them as a sign on your hand, and they shall be as frontlets between your eyes. You shall write them on the doorposts of your house and on your gates. (Deuteronomy 6:4-9)

Chapter Three • *Confronting the Problem*

- I have not sat with idolatrous mortals,
  Nor will I go in with hypocrites.
  I have hated the assembly of evildoers,
  And will not sit with the wicked. (Psalm 26:4-5)
- Whoever has no rule over his own spirit
  Is like a city broken down, without walls. (Proverbs 25:28)

Some choir members can't wait until they finish the last song before they start tipping and sneaking out the back door. If you can't stand to spend an extra five minutes in worship, how will you cope with an eternity in heaven?

- A good name is better than precious ointment,
  And the day of death than the day of one's birth;
  Better to go to the house of mourning
  Than to go to the house of feasting,
  For that is the end of all men;
  And the living will take it to heart.
  Sorrow is better than laughter,
  For by a sad countenance the heart is made better.
  The heart of the wise is in the house of mourning,
  But the heart of fools is in the house of mirth.
  It is better to hear the rebuke of the wise
  Than for a man to hear the song of fools.
  For like the crackling of thorns under a pot,
  So is the laughter of the fool.
  This also is vanity.
  Surely oppression destroys a wise man's reason,
  And a bribe debases the heart.
  The end of a thing is better than its beginning;
  The patient in spirit is better than the proud in spirit.
  Do not hasten in your spirit to be angry,
  For anger rests in the bosom of fools.

Do not say,
"Why were the former days better than these?"
For you do not inquire wisely concerning this.
Wisdom is good with an inheritance,
And profitable to those who see the sun.
For wisdom is a defense as money is a defense,
But the excellence of knowledge is that wisdom gives life to those who have it.
Consider the work of God;
For who can make straight what He has made crooked?
In the day of prosperity be joyful,
But in the day of adversity consider:
Surely God has appointed the one as well as the other,
So that man can find out nothing that will come after him.
(Ecclesiastes 7:1-14)

- And when a great multitude had gathered, and they had come to Him from every city, He spoke by a parable: "A sower went out to sow his seed. And as he sowed, some fell by the wayside; and it was trampled down, and the birds of the air devoured it. Some fell on rock; and as soon as it sprang up, it withered away because it lacked moisture. And some fell among thorns, and the thorns sprang up with it and choked it. But others fell on good ground, sprang up, and yielded a crop a hundredfold." When He had said these things He cried, "He who has ears to hear, let him hear!" Then His disciples asked Him, saying, "What does this parable mean?" And He said, "To you it has been given to know the mysteries of the kingdom of God, but to the rest it is given in parables, that ' Seeing they may not see, And hearing they may not understand.'
"Now the parable is this: The seed is the word of God. Those by the wayside are the ones who hear; then the devil

comes and takes away the word out of their hearts, lest they should believe and be saved. But the ones on the rock are those who, when they hear, receive the word with joy; and these have no root, who believe for a while and in time of temptation fall away. Now the ones that fell among thorns are those who, when they have heard, go out and are choked with cares, riches, and pleasures of life, and bring no fruit to maturity. But the ones that fell on the good ground are those who, having heard the word with a noble and good heart, keep it and bear fruit with patience. (Luke 8:4-15)

Point Nine: Do not indulge in loud talking or jesting after the service is concluded.

Raucous or coarse conversations are always out of order, especially in the aftermath of worshiping God. Ideally we carry the blessing of worship with us into the trials and struggles of the week. What does it say about us, if we move from reverence to rowdiness in a matter of moments? If you must speak with someone, do it with a polite and respectful attitude. Go to an individual privately and never talk loudly or be involved in fault-finding with another.

Point Ten: Let reverence be the keyword.

The church must demand this often neglected quality. If worship and the House of God are to be respected, they must be honored at all times. The presence of the Lord always calls for our utmost respect.

One important aspect of this respect is the behavior of visiting deacons, licensed ministers, and church leaders. Rather than seeking personal honor, such persons must remember that they have been ordained and appointed only in their home congregation. If visiting deacons attend worship, they are to sit in the pews, as do all other worshipers. If the deacon or licensed minister is recognized by one of the church leaders and then invited to the front or to a designated seat, only then may the visitor come forward. Proper reverence teaches us to disregard our own honor for the sake of devotion.

Point Eleven: Bring a spirit of loving encouragement to worship.

During prayer, all heads should be bowed and all eyes closed. Say "Amen" during the prayer as the Spirit leads. At the end of the prayer, your "Amen" affirms the prayer and claims it as your own offering to God.

Say "Amen" to the preached word to encourage the preacher and to witness to the truth of God's word. Many excuse themselves from this verbal response with the nodding of the head. The polite and sincere nodding of one's head is no substitute for making a joyful noise unto the Lord. Too many of our churches condone a style of worship that is more conducive to a good nap than Spirit-filled praise. Though nodding the head may be a sincere gesture, the Scripture says, "Let the redeemed of the Lord say so." (Psalm 107:2)

> COMPLAINERS ARE MISERABLE PEOPLE AND MISERY LOVES COMPANY.

The worship time is not the period to critically analyze the music, the sermon, or the praying. I have seen people sit in church with pen or pencil circling errors and misprints in the bulletin. They gloat whenever the speaker misuses a verb or mispronounces a word. They gleefully seize on the mistake each time a singer wanders off-key or a musician plays the wrong note.

Complainers are miserable people and misery loves company. These carping critics entirely miss the true meaning and purpose of worship, which is more concerned with praising than performing. In

Chapter Three • *Confronting the Problem*

my own experience, I have seen an untutored singer with an unexceptional voice move a congregation more deeply than others who deem themselves outstanding in vocal skill and training. The difference lies in the presence of the Spirit. The Spirit of the Lord comes when the church is of one accord. When the church prays and seeks God's face, then will we hear from heaven. Many of our churches never experience God because "That which is born of the flesh is flesh, and that which is born of the Spirit is spirit." (John 3:6)

> DON'T SIT SMUGLY IN THE CHURCH BEING SO "SPIRITUAL" THAT YOU MISS THE SPIRIT WHEN HE COMES.

Through the years, I have seen ministers who worship with sour faces, giving no hint of encouragement to the preacher. On the other hand, if they personally like the preacher, they act as if that makes the preacher's message a more powerful and genuine expression of God's word.

We must cease this foolishness. "Do not be deceived, God is not mocked; for whatever a man sows, that he will also reap." (Galatians 6:7) The most critical persons in the church hide their own personal insecurities by attacking others. They loudly criticize, but they never achieve the same mark or accomplishments of the person they attack.

I do not advocate becoming a pulpit or pew cheerleader for the sake of making noise. However, just as you encourage the child who is learning or attempting to do his/her best, so brothers and sisters should encourage each other.

Perhaps the preacher is not a powerful orator. Maybe the choir is not the best in town, singing the top ten. Nevertheless, an encouraging "Amen," a friendly smile and a positive response lift up the service and the worshipers. Don't sit smugly in the church being so "spiritual" that you miss the Spirit when He comes.

Criticizing the preacher undermines effectiveness in the pulpit. The Bible acknowledges as much when God tells Jeremiah, "Therefore prepare yourself and arise, and speak to them all that I command you. Do not be dismayed before their faces, lest I dismay you before them." (Jeremiah 1:17) Conversely, encouraging the preacher leads to better preaching. This positive interaction between pew and pulpit is the beauty of the African-American church.

Allow me to offer a word to ministers. Always strive for a good and wholesome relationship with your pastor and church members. If another church is considering you for a pastoral or staff position, do not pursue that conversation in secret. In every case, the pulpit committee, the officers and the members of the new church will call your church of membership for a reference. If you are uncooperative and have a stormy relationship with your pastor and home church, you will probably bring the same problems to a new church.

Leaders who sleep or "rest their eyes" while sitting in the pew, especially on the front row, dishearten the church. Such behavior suggests, especially to children and guests, that the worship is neither important nor interesting—so wake me when it's over.

- Then He came to the disciples and found them sleeping, and said to Peter, "What! Could you not watch with Me one hour? Watch and pray, lest you enter into temptation. The spirit indeed is willing, but the flesh is weak."
  Again, a second time, He went away and prayed, saying, "O My Father, if this cup cannot pass away from Me unless I drink it, Your will be done." And He came and found them asleep again, for their eyes were heavy.
  So He left them, went away again, and prayed the third time, saying the same words. Then He came to His disciples and said to them, "Are you still sleeping and resting? Behold, the hour is at hand, and the Son of Man is

being betrayed into the hands of sinners. Rise, let us be going. See, My betrayer is at hand." (Matthew 26:40-46)
- The woman said to Him, "Sir, I perceive that You are a prophet. Our fathers worshiped on this mountain, and you Jews say that in Jerusalem is the place where one ought to worship."
Jesus said to her, "Woman, believe Me, the hour is coming when you will neither on this mountain, nor in Jerusalem, worship the Father. You worship what you do not know; we know what we worship, for salvation is of the Jews. But the hour is coming, and now is, when the true worshipers will worship the Father in spirit and truth; for the Father is seeking such to worship Him. God is Spirit, and those who worship Him must worship in spirit and truth."
(John 4:19-24)
- As cold water to a weary soul,
So is good news from a far country.
A righteous man who falters before the wicked
Is like a murky spring and a polluted well.
It is not good to eat much honey;
So to seek one's own glory is not glory.
Whoever has no rule over his own spirit
Is like a city broken down, without walls.
(Proverbs 25:25-28)

For political reasons, some people are placed in charge of seminars, workshops and lecture series even though haven't attended Sunday School or Christian education sessions in years. Appointing such ill-equipped people to positions of authority dishonors both the work and the workers of the church.
- Be diligent to present yourself approved to God, a worker who does not need to be ashamed, rightly dividing the word of truth. (II Timothy 2:15)

- You search the Scriptures, for in them you think you have eternal life; and these are they which testify of Me. (John 5:39)

Point Twelve: Always dress modestly as becomes Christians.

We have saved for last a potentially controversial matter. The whole discussion of proper dress and attire raises a long-standing debate in the body of Christ. For instance, some churches do not allow women to wear makeup, open-toe shoes, pants/slacks, or short dresses. These prohibitions unfairly target women and such regulations are rarely biblical. Modesty should not be a pretext for creating arbitrary standards for the dress and grooming of others.

Not that make-up or hemlines are the only issues at stake in this discussion. Consider the ongoing debate about wearing uniforms in public schools. Private and parochial schools have long followed this practice. From across the country, we hear reports of young men and women losing their lives because their clothes are stolen off their backs. Designer labels and expensive jewelry have aggravated this situation. As a parent, I know that tennis shoes, jackets, and designer-label clothing are expensive. What is the Christian response to these problems?

Peer pressure drives us to buy what we don't need to impress folks we don't like with money we don't have. Unfortunately, peer pressure is also present in the church. We have all heard people excuse themselves from worship because they do not have the proper clothes to wear.

With thoughtful planning and careful purchasing, most church members in this country can build a respectable, attractive wardrobe that maintains Christian standards of modesty and self-respect without chasing the current fad.

As a starting point, every minister, church officer and lay leader needs to own a black suit or dress with a white shirt or blouse. This standard attire, completed by black shoes and socks (or appropriate stocking for ladies) serves for weddings, Communion services, funerals, banquets and semi-formal dinners. If you are extremely visible as a church leader, you may be wise to include navy blue, white, and off-white outfits.

In my opinion, church leaders should dress conservatively. Professional dress during service times and church functions is always acceptable. Avoid loud, flashy, and trendy clothing. Not every style sold in the store is appropriate for ministers and church leaders. Some styles are not even appropriate for members to wear. Many fashions are a poor fit for the builds of African-American men and women. They are European or Italian cut, not African-American cut. We look stuffed and uncomfortable in these clothes, like five pounds of pork in a three-pound sausage skin.

Good taste and common sense should guide our choice of clothing. I take it as a compliment when I am dressed casually and someone asks, "Are you a minister?" Always dress in a manner appropriate for a representative of Christ and His Church. Although this is not the current trend, the minister nevertheless needs to be tastefully dressed, yet know he is not advertising clothing, but rather Christ.

Several years ago I bumped into a very noted pastor in my city in the men's clothing section of a store in an outlet mall. We exchanged greetings and commiserated that we were limited in our selections due to our respective sizes. I noticed one black suit that would fit this pastor, and I lifted it to his chest for him and his wife to inspect. He admitted that he did not own a black suit, and at my urging he left the store with that suit under his arm. Each time I have encountered this pastor over the last twenty years, he has thanked me for that advice. He tells me that he has worn that black suit to countless functions and he always receives compliments.

Every minister needs a black suit. Green and red lizard shoes with a purple suit may have their place, but I would not want a minister wearing loud, psychedelic colors while standing over the remains of my loved one or performing the wedding for my daughter. More importantly, the carriers of the Word, the presenters of the gospel, should take great concern in the clothes they wear as they serve the people of God.

Some will disagree, but whether we like it or not, a tasteless or brassy style of dress undermines a minister's professionalism. Always be dignified in your dress. Wear the best clothes your budget can afford. Buy the latest style if you wish, but avoid public display. A minister should be admired for what resides in the head and heart rather than what rides on the back. In ministry and in life, the contents are far more important than the packaging.

In this discussion of grooming and style, we should address jewelry as well. Church members who wish may wear jewelry without qualms as long as they exercise good taste and restraint. A person adorned with three earrings in each ear and four chains draped around the neck is neither restrained nor tasteful. Unless one is trying out for the film role of Ringo Starr, a ring on every finger is excessive. Too much gold shining on the teeth creates a smile that resembles Christmas decorations. To paraphrase the Greek philosopher, "Moderation in all things—especially precious metals!"

Those who act in an official capacity should be even more conservative in choosing jewelry and accessories. Keep decorative eyeglasses, large bracelets, and noticeable jewelry to a minimum. A little sparkle goes a long way. Choir members, ushers, nurses, officers, and ministers should wear little, if any, jewelry while serving the church. When and if it is worn, it should be done in uniform only and not with one individual standing out and drawing attention to himself.

Originally clergy and choir wore robes to cover the person and the position held in daily life. Ideally worship robes obscure the leaders so that all our attention may be given to God. For this reason, we never pin flowers, corsages or boutonnieres on robes. Unfortunately we often thwart the theology of the robe by decorating our vestments with symbols to display our achievements and earn recognition.

Women should avoid tight pants and blue jeans. Some churches feel that women should not wear pants at all, especially in the church. I feel that if the pants men and women wear are two sizes too small, they are inappropriate for public and church functions. The purpose of the church is to lift up Christ, not the flesh.

Female ministers now serve many of our churches. These ministers should always remember that ministry extends beyond Sunday morning. Women in ministry must always dress modestly. In the pulpit, knee length dresses or skirts are appropriate. I recall the spectacle of a sister in a very short dress who kept pulling on it throughout the service in hopes of covering herself. I wanted to say to the lady, "Stop pulling on your dress, because you don't have any more to pull."

If a woman's hemline is sensible, she does not need to cover her knees with a fancy lace handkerchief that just happens to match the outfit. In short, choose worship clothing with discretion and common sense. Men and women should dress properly when seated in the pulpit, for they draw every eye in the church. Church leaders should model Christian grooming habits, not garish billboards or glamour magazine covers.

SUCCESSFUL DRESSING

Guidelines for both Men and Women, written by The Fulton County Extension Service (1983).

Suggestions for Men

- A two or three-piece suit idea is always appropriate. A nice shirt and tie makes this a smart outfit.
- Do have your ankles covered. Wear socks that are mid-calf length at least. Socks should stay up; those with worn elastic should be tossed or fixed.
- Do wear a tie. Do not have your collar lying open.
- Keep shirts tucked inside your pants.
- Shave as often as needed. A 5 o'clock shadow at 9 a.m. is out.
- Check out the dress codes. Jeans are not proper to wear everywhere. If jeans are permitted, be sure they're neat, clean, mended, and not too broken in.
- Jogging pants are too casual. A dressier pair of pants looks better.
- Trade in your worn sneakers for a great pair of loafers or string-up oxfords.

Suggestions for Women

- Wear medium heeled shoes that have a closed toe or narrow opening at the toe.
- Wear an under-slip that is the right length and does not show. A slip that's too long looks plain sloppy and a blouse you can see through without a slip or camisole underneath is worse.
- Wear just one bangle bracelet, too many will clang.

- Easy on any jewelry, a few pieces of jewelry play up an outfit. Too much can detract. When in doubt, remove one piece.
- Hose should be a natural color, maybe a shade darker than your skin tone. No bright colors and no snags or runs.
- Ladies, makeup can make you look terrific—if you wear it the right way! Not too much! It should look natural and well blended.
- The outfit should make you look serious. If you're looking for attention, you'll get it in a low-cut dress. Save the party outfit for after hours. Avoid extremes.
- Pants shouldn't be too tight, and not too baggy.
- Find the right skirt length for you. You don't have to change with the tides. Just below the knee is good for most ladies and most activities.

SUMMARY OF THE TWELVE POINTS

The following brief summary of the Twelve Points may be helpful as a quick reference for readers who wish a review.

Point One	**Be on time.**
Point Two	**Never pass up the aisle during prayer or Scripture reading.**
Point Three	**Show respect for the worship service.**
Point Four	**Be devout in every attitude.**
Point Five	**Be thoughtful of the comfort of others.**
Point Six	**Be a welcoming committee of one.**
Point Seven	**Properly address the pulpit and church body.**
Point Eight	**Depart from the church as reverently as you entered.**

Point Nine	**Do not indulge in loud talking or jesting after the service is concluded.**
Point Ten	**Let reverence be the keyword.**
Point Eleven	**Bring a spirit of loving encouragement to worship.**
Point Twelve	**Always dress modestly as becomes Christians.**

A HIGHER STANDARD INSIDE AND OUT

We may conclude our discussion with one further thought about dress and grooming. One cannot step outdoors without being forcefully reminded that tasteful standards of dress have all but disappeared in our culture. Anything goes these days: any amount of exposed flesh, any offensive motto on a T-shirt, any gaudy display of jewelry, any cut of slacks, any hemline.

If such dubious fashions are acceptable in the world, why should the church oppose the trend? Simply put, the church is called to love the people of the world, but we are not called to become the world. We are the people of God, the family of Christ. As I have demonstrated again and again in this book, Christians live by a different standard. That standard should be especially evident in worship and at church events.

> CHRISTIANS LIVE BY A DIFFERENT STANDARD.

The prophet Zechariah describes a striking vision that speaks to our hearts. He sees a court convened in heaven and the high priest Joshua, representing the people of Israel, stands accused before God. Israel's deep sin is represented by the filthy, tattered clothing in which Joshua is dressed. The prosecuting attorney is Satan himself. Imagine Joshua's despair and hopelessness as he stands in the heavenly court wrapped in dirty rags, ashamed before God and threatened by Satan.

But the loving God intervenes, overrules Satan's accusations, and declares Joshua forgiven. Here's how Zechariah tells the story. Take careful note of what happens after Joshua is vindicated by God.

"Then he showed me Joshua the high priest standing before the Angel of the LORD, and Satan standing at his right hand to oppose him. And the LORD said to Satan, 'The LORD rebuke you, Satan! The LORD who has chosen Jerusalem rebuke you! Is this not a brand plucked from the fire?'

Now Joshua was clothed with filthy garments, and was standing before the Angel.

Then He answered and spoke to those who stood before Him, saying, 'Take away the filthy garments from him.' And to him He said, 'See, I have removed your iniquity from you, and I will clothe you with rich robes.'

And I said, 'Let them put a clean turban on his head.'

So they put a clean turban on his head, and they put the clothes on him."

The story reminds us how much God has done for you and me. Purely by grace and the blood of Christ, God has stripped off our filthy unrighteousness and clothed us in salvation and love. This is why Christians live by a higher standard, so that we can express our gratitude to the God who saved us. We practice habits of respect and reverence so that God can take pleasure in us and see our sincere gratitude.

As we choose our clothes for worship, perhaps we should consider this: If God has clothed us with holiness on the *inside*, surely we can dress accordingly on the *outside*.

PART TWO:
ORDER IN THE PULPIT

4

SEEKING THE VISION

WHEN THERE IS NO VISION

Thus far we have examined church etiquette and behavior from the perspective of those who fill the pews. We have considered the responsibilities and privileges of church membership and God's calling to order and mutual respect within the family of believers. Our exploration of the biblical vision of the church reveals God's plan for a transformative family of faith in which each member plays a significant role in serving and honoring our Lord.

In the latter half of this book we now turn our attention to the front of the sanctuary and focus particularly upon ministerial standards of etiquette. We lightly touched upon this topic earlier and now we will pursue the matter in more depth. The behavior of ministers is important both for its own sake and also for the model ministers present to the church at large. The shepherd must abide by even higher standards than those required of the flock. Just as God calls for order among church members in general, our Lord zealously requires order in the pulpit as well.

Before we address the practical nuts and bolts of ministerial etiquette, we will lay down a theological framework for our thinking. Pastoral behavior is more than a list of rules; it is an effort to "live out" our Christian beliefs within the context of church leadership. To help sketch a theology of ministry, I will begin by sharing a systematic and biblical understanding of my personal practice of ministry.

> THE BEHAVIOR OF MINISTERS IS IMPORTANT

I offer this personal view of ministry for two reasons. First, I believe my vision of ministry, hammered out through years of experience, prayer, reflection, and study, may yield helpful insights to other ministers struggling with similar issues in the pastorate.

Second—and more important—I hope my own reflections will encourage other pastors to clarify and articulate their particular perspectives on ministry. Even if you don't agree with everything I have to say, I hope to convince you of the crucial importance of careful and prayerful expression of your theological framework for serving God in the church. I humbly present my vision as a working model of the kind of vision every pastor ought to formulate.

As God's appointed leader in the congregation, the pastor has a responsibility to inspire his staff and colleagues with his or her personal vision for that particular church. If each pastor had a written outline of the assumptions and beliefs undergirding God's work, many churches would escape the turmoil and conflict associated with clashing priorities and differing styles.

Before deciding to become a part of a local church, the wise minister will seek to clearly understand and devoutly accept the mission of that church and the vision of the pastor. A straightforward statement of ministry goals and practices allows a prospective minister to make a thoughtful and informed determination about whether God he has a calling to that particular congregation.

With hundreds, even thousands, of churches in most cities, no minister needs to settle for being miserable in the service of a congregation that doesn't match his own vision and calling. When the minister is mismatched with the congregation—or the pastor—the outcome leads to conflict and bad feelings.

> PASTORAL BEHAVIOR IS MORE THAN A LIST OF RULES...

Serving Christ is sufficiently challenging without complicating the practice of ministry with hidden agendas, squabbling for special attention, jockeying for position, maneuvering to preach, and competing for the favor of the pastor or some other church leader. When infighting prevails, bitterness, confusion, and frustration hamstring our work on God's behalf.

Having seen first-hand the sad aftermath of such church conflicts, I encourage every pastor to draft and communicate a personal vision of the meaning and method of ministry within the local church. Only with shared vision is shared leadership possible in the congregation. To that end, I offer my own vision of Christian ministry as a model for consideration by other pastors.

THE BLACK BIRTHRIGHT

Black Americans are born into a complicated and ambiguous heritage. Only a few decades ago I joined many of my peers in cursing my birthright as a member of the Negroid race. Yet the African-American experience also yielded unexpected blessings. Although growing up black in America was difficult, our parents and community taught us to savor the uniquely rich and valuable minority experience. As we came to terms with our racial identity, our elders continually told us, "You can be somebody!" Regardless of how the majority culture might view us, there was a rich future awaiting those who were sufficiently determined to seize it.

Indeed, our value as persons was well established. Not only could I become somebody *someday*, I was already somebody *today*. The love that surrounded me affirmed my identity independent of social and economic disadvantages. I treasure the childhood experience of togetherness in the midst of cultural apartness. I do not glorify poverty, but I give thanks for the spirit of a community that faced financial need with playfulness, the expectation of deliverance, and the gospel message that "trouble can't last always."

> ONLY WITH SHARED VISION IS SHARED LEADERSHIP POSSIBLE...

Those encouraging words nurtured my spirit through hard times. "You are somebody," my parents told me over and over. Their certainty allowed me to see my worth through their eyes. "And you're going to be somebody in the eyes of the world," they promised. The courage exemplified by such attitudes enabled struggling, grade-school educated parents to rear a family on fifty dollars a week to become somebody in America. I am that somebody.

My perception of ministry is shaped largely by where I have been. When I think of the role of the minister, my first impression grows from the black ministers who fed my soul through my maturing years in the 1950's and 1960's. My understanding of the pastoral role emerges from my experiences in the black church. In most black communities, the ministry was the first and often the only profession to gain a foothold in society.

Because I realized the awesome task of the minister, especially the black minister, the contemplation of accepting a call into the ministry was a tremendous decision. In my thinking, a minister is simply someone who serves Christ through the church, whether or not that person is specially educated and ordained. For instance, we commonly speak of Youth Ministers and Ministers of Music without assuming theological education or ordination. Referring to the ordained clergy as "minister" does not defrock others who serve in different capacities. Therefore, minister is a general term describing anyone who ministers or serves: clergy, ordained, commissioned, or set apart by the church to a particular task.

To clarify the distinction, the professional clergy is a formally trained and ordained minister of a church or denomination. The Baptist Church from which I received my early Christian education recognized both ministers and professional clergy. Our pastor was one of the few trained black pastors in the city of Nashville. Consequently, as I pondered my calling from God, I had to decide if I would accept the responsibility and challenge of becoming a "minister" or a "professional clergy."

MODELS OF MINISTRY

When I made my decision to enter the professional ministry, the only model of ministry available to me was Dubois' ideal of the smiling politician who preached and exhibited a pleasant personality. I fully expected to be the boss in my congregation, the unchallenged leader of the pack. These preconceived ideas were easier to cultivate before I delivered my first sermon or "ministered" to anyone.

My narrow-minded opinion of the ministry expanded when the scriptural passage from Luke 4:18 became my burning testimony: "The Spirit of the Lord is upon me, because he hath anointed me to preach the gospel..." I interpreted the work of preaching very fundamentally, narrowly, and charismatically. God was calling me to stand over the ditch of life and lift my poor fallen brothers and sisters from despair, restoring their sight and delivering them from the oppressor, Lucifer himself. In other words, my life was in order and I intended to help others get their lives in order, too. I could point the way because I had already arrived!

If my earlier attitude smacks of self-righteousness, I can only plead the naiveté of youth and honest sincerity. Of course, a person may be absolutely sincere and still be altogether wrong. Fortunately, God was patient with me. Through the years, I have changed my thinking about the nature of my calling, but I have never doubted the calling itself. As surely as God summoned Amos from Tekoa and laid a hand upon the youthful Jeremiah and appeared to Isaiah in the temple and seized Paul on the Damascus road, so also God set me aside for the ministry.

> THE TASK OF MINISTRY SHOULD EXTEND BEYOND THE ORGANIZED CHURCH

Although I had no doubt about God's call, I kept raising the issue, "What kind of minister will I be?" My one-sided approach to ministry grew increasingly inadequate as I considered how little training and experience I brought to my calling. The writing of Urban T. Holmes has been a Godsend in expanding my understanding of ministry. According to Holmes, the priest or minister serves both the community and God. This role does not undermine but furthers the priesthood of all believers. All Christians are ministers, but the power of the priestly office expresses itself in every religious community, even in cases without a formal leader. Every religious community chooses someone explicitly or implicitly to fulfill the necessary function of the priest.

While the Lucan passage mentioned earlier remains my biblical starting point, I contend that the task of ministry should extend beyond the organized church into the larger community. Shifting the focus of my calling from self to community was a difficult transition, turning upside-down many long-cherished beliefs. In search of guidance and training, I enrolled part-time at a small black Baptist Bible college while working as an engineer for South Central Bell Telephone Company. God provided the further guidance that later led me to surrender my engineering career to enter the professional ministry full time. To that end I entered Candler School of Theology to broaden my theological perception and purpose in ministry.

EASY ANSWERS?

As part of my seminary education, I worked at the Fulton County Alcoholism Treatment Center, on Boulevard Avenue, near downtown Atlanta. In that setting I encountered the raw wounds of human need. Dealing with the ragged edge of life soon convinced me that pat answers and canned ideas were inadequate to the challenges of ministry. One day as I mingled with patients at the center, a young man drew me aside for a heart-rending conversation. This handsome man in his late twenties confessed that his struggle with homosexuality had driven him to alcoholism. In the church of his upbringing he learned that all sex outside of marriage was sinful. Piously, I bowed my head in agreement and asked, "What have you done to deal with the problem of homosexuality as it confronts you?"

"I got married," he told me, "hoping to change my sexual feelings. I even had a son, but nothing changed inside me. The marriage fell apart. After the divorce, I went to a psychiatrist, still trying to change my feelings."

"Did that help?" I asked.

"No," he said bitterly. "I ended up having sex with the psychiatrist. I became so disgusted with myself that I withdrew from everyone and everything. I lived like a hermit. In my loneliness, I turned to alcohol for comfort. As if I didn't have enough problems already, now I'm trying to stay clean and sober."

He leaned forward and fixed his eyes on mine.

"Reverend, what do I do with this thing that is so deep inside me? Did God make me a freak? Can't God make me a heterosexual?"

I groped for words that wouldn't come. This desperate and wretched young man needed to hear more than the Scriptures I had previously recited denouncing homosexuality. I felt that his exposure to the church and his experience of Scripture had brought him more pain than healing. When that conversation ended, I walked away feeling utterly inadequate to deal with this situation. My King James magic charm gave no quick and easy answer for the struggle erupting in this man's soul.

At this point, I began to seriously examine and challenge my previous perspective, exploring new dimensions of ministry. To borrow the terminology of James Hopewell, I had to leave the faun, the line separating the sacred and the profane. Through my continuing studies, I settled on four constants in ministry:

1. Identification: to identify and understand who I am and what I stand for;
2. Integration: to integrate morale within the congregation and to evaluate how we stand together;
3. Adoption: to embrace ministry within an ever-changing community and environment;
4. Goal attainment: to realize both the church's purpose and my purpose as minister.

5

LAYING THE FOUNDATION

THEOLOGICAL FOUNDATION FOR MINISTRY

Because my experience in the institutional church has exerted such a formative influence on my theology, through much of my ministry I have struggled to define the place and purpose of the church. We must be clear about our own theology of the church in order to embrace those who seek to understand its purpose.

The meaning of the church is inseparable from its mission. The writing of J. Deotis Roberts, a black theologian and President of Interdenominational Theological Center in Atlanta, offers a three-fold model for the calling of the church. According to Roberts, the church must first function as an extended family. Second, the church must use its power to challenge oppression. Third, the church must remind people of their own sins and responsibilities. Roberts specifically addresses the black church, but I contend that his ideas embody the mission of the whole church. The mission of the contemporary church emerges from the very nature of the gospel.

Roberts' ideas resonate with my personal experience. I have experienced the church first and foremost as a living community. The relational aspect of the church is vital to understanding the other qualities of the church. "Community" is a broad term that might describe many non-church gatherings, so I will offer a more specific definition of the term. The church is a community or fellowship of persons who believe in the power of redemption through the life, death, and resurrection of Jesus Christ. Scripture implies that where two or more are gathered in fellowship in the name of Jesus, the church is present.

> THE CHURCH IS A COMMUNITY OF PERSONS WHO ENCOUNTER JESUS THROUGH ENCOUNTERING EACH OTHER.

The church informs the experience of black human existence within a Christian context. The black congregation often provides the only continuity and solidarity for the black community itself. Cone says the black church was born out of protest. He acknowledges that "fellowship with God" is the beginning and the end of human liberation. The black church provides a community wherein the people gather to experience the truth of their existence as lived together by God's Spirit.

THE LIBERATED COMMUNITY

Due to slavery and continuing inhumane treatment the black person had nowhere to turn except the church. Major black religious leaders like Richard Allen, Daniel Payne, Henry Highland Garnet,

Nat Turner, and Martin Luther King, Jr. addressed the spiritual as well as social, economic, and political dimensions of reality from within the black church. The Sunday gathering of "the saints" was the only place "old Jim" or "the nigger" was considered human. Calling one another "Brother" and "Sister" expressed both full humanity and respect absent from the black experience in the prevailing culture. This gathered community redefined humanity, overturning the humiliation, oppression and false judgment that ruled the other six days of the week.

Worship was not exclusively a political event, but also an eschatological happening. Worship offered a glimpse of the Kingdom of God. The self-affirming nature of the church offers stability and unity found in no other gathering. In other words, the church provides a sense of worthiness and confirms the inherent dignity of human life. The church is a community of persons who encounter Jesus through encountering each other.

Worship depends entirely on the Spirit who descends upon the gathered community. The divine Spirit is not merely a metaphysical entity, but rather the power of Jesus breaking into human life. The Spirit grants a new song as confirmation of God's presence with Christians engaged in a historical struggle. The presence of the divine Spirit accounts for the intensity of worship in the black tradition. The Spirit energizes the rhythm of song and sermon, the passion of prayer, the communal joy of testimony, the ecstasy of shout and conversion as the people project their humanity in the togetherness of the Spirit.

How, then, is this divine Spirit at work among the lives of those who make up the church? Are we experiencing an incarnate presence or a spiritual reality? Throughout human history, God has intervened in our lives. In the person of Jesus Christ, God took on humanity. Although still divine, God revealed Himself in a unique and lasting way through human flesh. This incarnation of God resulted in our redemption.

The source of humanity's uniqueness, that which distinguishes us from all other created objects, is our creation in the image of God. In the fall, the image of God's image—the *imago dei*—was lost to human relationships, but in the incarnation, humanity and divinity are united to its true nature. This incarnate presence of the Spirit not only unites the individual, but also all those who allow themselves to be transformed by encountering the Spirit. That Spirit meets us as we gather in the community and fellowship of worshipers. Further, the Spirit calls us to be instruments of God as He liberates the oppressed.

THE LIVING STORY

The early Christian community encountered Christ in the stories of those who knew Him first-hand. Storytelling is a significant part of the church, particularly the black church. Often a person in the "amen corner" of the black church encourages the preacher by exclaiming, "Tell the story." Vocal encouragement from the congregation tells the preacher that he or she is on the right track. A chorus of scattered voices declaring "Amen!" affirms that the preacher's words ring true to the Spirit's presence in the midst of the people.

If the people do not say "Amen" or give some other passionate response, we assume the Spirit has chosen not to speak through the preacher at that time. The absence of the Spirit could mean that the preacher was too dependent on his or her own wisdom or eloquence. In the black church, an "Amen" involves the people in the proclamation and commits them to the divine truth announced in preaching, testimony, and song. Through stories shared in worship, members of the congregation encounter the man Jesus.

Story is the foundation of Christian unity. The church lives by

Chapter Five • *Laying the Foundation*

an inherited story when we acknowledge as Savior the one who taught by story. Paul Tillich's theology of sign and symbol suggests the central importance of story in the Christian tradition. Tillich believes that all language about God is symbolic. We cannot judge a story simply in terms of its literal truth or falsehood. Stories carry meaning far beyond the actual words.

Images emerge from our stories and take on a life of their own. Some of these images may be unhealthy and alienating, such as the implied picture of a white, blond-haired, blue-eyed Jesus, a depiction understandably difficult for people of color to accept or understand. Thus, Karl Barth warns that any attempt to interpret Jesus as the Christ can lead conceptually to an actual denial of the Christ-character of Jesus. The symbols Son of Man, Son of God, the Christ, and the Word—the *Logos*—are necessary, but by themselves these concepts are inadequate interpretations of the Christian message. Further, Barth sees the church as a group called together through the revealed word of Christ. The church begins with the story and then relates to the realities of life. Tillich similarly views the church as a relational body professing Christ and the continuing presence of the Holy Spirit.

> THE CHURCH IS A COMMUNITY PROCLAIMING THE REVEALED WORD OF GOD.

The community shares symbols, images, and stories through professing Christ biblically, historically, and personally. This communal sharing liberates and heals. In part, the liberation emerges through realizing the commonality of our alienation. The Bible stories share in this persistent sense of aloneness. Sharing the brokenness of one's personal story relates to the brokenness of the community and the brokenness of Christ. Yet the Christ story offers the hope of resurrection. Within the church, we celebrate this hope not only in words but also in breaking bread together.

Barth is undoubtedly correct when he says the church is a community proclaiming the revealed word of God. However, I wish to carry Barth's thinking a step further. The church is the community living and acting out the revealed word of God. The church is a community of persons encountering Jesus Christ through the Spirit and acting out of the Christ story.

SHALOM AND RECONCILIATION

A true sense of the whole gospel—that God's son died in the world for the world—awakens the desire for "shalom." The Hebrew word shalom is often translated as peace, but the whole meaning of the word is more far-reaching. Shalom is the life-giving agent through which the blind receive their sight, the lame walk, the dead rise up, and the poor have the good news preached to them (Luke 4:18). The concept of shalom encourages a broad, immense vision of liberation and reconciliation among God, humanity, and nature. In that redeemed world, all the fractures are finally healed: between man and God, man and man, man and nature, within nature, and among man, nature, and God.

Cynics may deride the gospel promise as pious rhetoric, but this message of shalom brings genuine hope to those in the spiritual and literal ghettos of life, those who reap injustice at the gain of the oppressor. Through the promised shalom of Christ, the poor find freedom to rebel and challenge every dehumanizing power and social structure. This is my understanding of the church's mission, particularly in the coming decade.

Some will object to my heavy emphasis on experience, an issue I will address later. For now, suffice it to say that I am trying to bridge the vast gap between my personal experience of the black church and the abstract theological language of European thinkers such as Barth and Tillich. I intentionally employ personal and individualistic language, even at the risk of misunderstanding by those who do not share my experience. Admittedly, my theology of the church—my ecclesiology—doesn't mesh well with the classical definition of the church handed down through the church fathers.

Rather than hide behind centuries-old traditional religious language and terminology, I prefer to build an ecclesiology that reflects the genuine and accessible experiences of contemporary black Christians. While I don't want to discard the old ways of talking about the church, I do want to offer a new way of thinking that will serve as an antidote to the "institutional self-deception" of the church. This self-deception has sometimes led the church to support slavery, segregation, colonialism, and Nazism while simultaneously proclaiming a so-called gospel in the name of Christ.

Tillich would contend that my doctrine of the church places too much emphasis on human liberation and meeting human need. I appreciate Tillich's reminder that even when all our material needs are met, we will still experience alienation and estrangement. On the other hand, I wonder if Tillich might be more inclined to believe that finite concern is "ultimate concern" if he were starving, enslaved, or unjustly imprisoned.

Another possible weakness of the experience-centered model is the lack of absolute appreciation for the institutional aspect of the church. The issue remains a struggle for me in my ministry. This reflects my idealism in questing for the "true community of God" or what Martin Luther King, Jr. called "the beloved community." Consequently, I see the community-centered approach providing a stronger base for outreach than reliance upon denominational boards.

THE KEY OF BLACK THEOLOGY

We have defined the church as the community living and acting out the revealed word of God in the power of the Spirit. Let me now turn our attention to the theology of liberation and how that belief shapes ministry. Nearly four decades have passed since Martin Luther King, Jr. was assassinated in Memphis, Tennessee. We are still dealing with the repercussions of King's espousal of "Black Theology." As articulated by Dr. King, Black Theology:

1. reinterprets God's relationship to the poor and oppressed and proclaims His activity in their liberation;
2. radically interprets Jesus as an oppressed person ministering to other victims of oppression;
3. views the poor and disenfranchised as sources of revelation of what God is doing in the world; and,
4. offers a new Christian witness, siding with the struggles of the poor and powerless.

In the effort to show that the gospel is political, black theologians sometimes reduce black religion to politics and black worship to a political strategy session, thereby distorting the essence of black religion. In spite of this danger, Black Theology offers a fresh and much-needed perspective on God's work in the world, a look at God's design through the eyes of those who dwell on the underside of society.

James Cone, an early proponent of Black Theology and Black Power, severely criticized white theologians for ignoring the plight of African-Americans. Cone outlined a theology to address the conditions and needs of black people. The efforts of thinkers like Cone prompted an enormous amount of literature relating theology to black religion and strategies for dealing with the social, economic, and political oppression of blacks. This literature made a significant contribution to theology by proclaiming that God's love and power are functioning among the oppressed for their salvation. In Black Theology, salvation cannot be

> ...ALL PERSONS MAY BE LIBERATED FROM PRECONCEIVED AND ILL-INFORMED MISCONCEPTIONS...

separated from liberation from dehumanizing life conditions. Instead of an otherworldly spirituality, Black Theology calls for Christians to fully respond to God's purposes for humanity.

In <u>Liberation and Reconciliation: A Black Theology and a Black Political Theology</u>, J. Deotis Roberts explores the interdependence between all people, especially black and white. Roberts goes further than Cone in stressing the interdependence between personal religious experience and community liberation. Roberts asserts that the ultimate goal of all human interaction is "reconciliation." One must allow for the uniqueness of the other and seek that all persons may be liberated from preconceived and ill-informed misconceptions about the other and affirm with all sincerity and dedication that Christ died for all humankind.

Not that Cone ignores reconciliation. In his book, <u>God of the Oppressed</u>, Cone maintains that "fellowship with God is the beginning of human liberation." Furthermore, fellowship with God is also the goal of human liberation. He notes that reconciliation with God is logically precedent to all other aspects of human liberation.

WHO AM I?

If Black Theology is to inform the liberation of black people, we require more writing and discourse to interpret how religious experience and spiritual development are significant to liberation. Why is religious experience so important to my theology, especially pertaining to liberation? Religious experience is the way to attain religious knowledge, and religious knowledge is necessary for liberation activities to proceed in accordance with God's will. Out of this experience the oppressed are "set at liberty."

Asking, "Who am I?" black Christians discover, "I am God's beloved one!"

Wondering, "What is my worth?" members of the community of faith find courage to declare, "I have ultimate worth."

Religious experience and liberation are inseparable. To support this thinking, I turn to Howard Thurman, the most prolific black theologian on this topic of religious experience. For over fifty years, he has expressed a deep commitment for remaking the social order. His work points to the inescapable fact that the destiny of the community is tied to the ability of individuals to have a "proper sense of self." This sense of self relates to and depends upon religious experience. For Thurman, religious experience is absolutely necessary in order to develop a theology that properly defines the humanity, political activity, and communal destiny of black people.

> RELIGIOUS EXPERIENCE PROVIDES ENERGY

In the work for liberation, fatigue may debilitate a community until it settles for lesser goals. Religious experience provides energy to meet the high calling and enormity of the challenge. Unless rooted in religious experience, the work of liberation and reconciliation will never realize its potential. Religious experience enables the oppressed to know that power is with them. They do not have to believe that the power is obtained through the use of the oppressor's weapons. Only non-violent power changes the very nature of the oppressor.

Martin Luther King, Jr. did not stay the course because he had studied Rauschenbusch's The Social Gospel. King's commitment to non-violence did not derive from his discipleship to DeWolf. King's defiant belief in the "beloved community" did not spring from Daddy King or Dr. Benjamin E. Mays. King was the leader of a powerful, liberating ministry in this land because of personal religious experience. Perhaps King himself could not articulate it, but he knew that a Spirit was at work within him, a Spirit greater than the spirit of the world.

> ONLY NON-VIOLENT POWER CHANGES THE VERY NATURE OF THE OPPRESSOR.

The old hymn captures the notion well:
…something within that holdeth the rein,
something within that vanishes pain,
something within that I cannot explain,
all that I know, there is something within.

Cone is correct when he claims that King's "dream" was grounded in nothing but God. King envisioned a new social order wherein all kinds of people and groups would live together as brothers and sisters much like the vision of the black church mentioned earlier.

Overemphasizing religious experience as the source of faith certainly has its perils. For instance, ecstasy may prove so satisfying that some Christians devote all their energies to an inner quest to achieve a "spiritual high" through meditation, worship, or contemplation. Such believers lose all grounding in history and politics, deciding that mystical experience is the only worthwhile reality. Others may lose the sense of interdependence with community and seek personal salvation to the exclusion of any social concern, as if finding a place in a distant heaven is more important than helping brothers and sisters in the present world.

> CHURCH AND COMMUNITY LACK THE PROPER LEADERSHIP AND DIRECTION

I conclude that the black church and community lack the proper leadership and direction because we attempt to perform the work of liberation without first receiving a liberating experience ourselves. Scripture says, "If the blind lead the blind they both shall fall into the ditch" (Matthew 15:14). It is the desire and purpose of my ministry to "preach the acceptable year of the Lord." After reading Cone, Roberts, Thurman, and King, I feel that this message will be preached in the church. If we are to be respected as liberation theologians in the midst of rising conservatism, we must raise up strong ministers of liberation for the new millennium.

6

ANSWERING THE CALL

A CALL TO MINISTRY

The letters of the apostle Paul typically deal with theology in the first half of the epistle and spend the second half applying that theology to the practical needs of everyday life. If I can't claim Paul's wisdom, at least I can emulate his style of writing. I have discussed at length the fundamental theology of Christian ministry. Now we turn our attention to the practice of ministry. In the pages that follow I will sketch an overview of sound procedures and offer guidelines for assuring that the shared ministry of the church is orderly and reasonable.

Traditionally, the Baptist Church has encouraged, equipped, and employed the service of persons called by God to preach the gospel of Jesus Christ. When one recognizes a calling to the ministry, the individual should publicly declare the call during the invitational period or at the opening of the doors of the church. This public testimony allows the pastor and congregation to acknowledge and bless the calling.

In order that the procedure may be orderly and respectful, everyone involved should scrupulously adhere to the order of the following guideline.

- The candidate makes an appointment with Pastor to acknowledge the call to the ministry.
- The candidate publicly acknowledges the call to ministry before the congregation.
- The pastor schedules the first sermon when h/she feels that the candidate has made adequate study, prayer, and preparation. Until the first sermon is delivered in the home church, the candidate for ministry is still considered a lay person. To be clear, there should be no pulpit assignments until after the first sermon.
- The candidate receives a license to preach the Gospel from his or her church following the first sermon.

The licensed preacher enters a period of training and further preparation under the supervision of the pastor. The church or pastor can revoke the license in the case of conduct unbecoming to a minister. The pastor will determine a date for ordination only after an appropriate time of oversight. The pastor maintains the responsibility for reviewing the candidate's commitment and service to the Lord, the Word, the church, and the work of the local congregation. During this time the pastor will clearly and intentionally share his theology of ministry and personal vision for the church so no confusion will arise about priorities and practices.

Until after ordination, a licensed minister cannot baptize, serve Communion, perform marriages, or bury the dead.

Chapter Six • *Answering the Call*

Answers to Frequently Asked Questions

Question: What does an individual do when he or she senses from the Holy Spirit a call to preach the gospel?

Answer: God calls every Christian to a holy purpose. Yet, we are especially privileged when God lays His hand on us, anoints our lips, and gives us a charge to spread the gospel. We dare not treat such a call lightly. At the first stirring of God's call, humbly approach the matter with an open spirit and a season of prayer.

If you feel this call on your life, you should:
- Immediately make an appointment with your pastor.
- Make no public announcements or testimonies of what God is doing for you.
- Silently observe and learn from other men and women of God who are strong role models.
- Wait on your calling. Even after meeting the risen Lord face to face on the Damascus Road, the apostle Paul spent three years in prayerful retreat and earnest study before beginning his public ministry. We should take his example to heart.

Question: What is my role as an associate minister at the church where I serve?

Answer: As an associate minister, your primary role is to actively and cheerfully support the Pastor in his effort to spiritually nurture the congregation. You can do this only through your steadfast commitment and loyalty to the kingdom of God.

Question: What does my certificate of license mean?

Answer: Your license grants you permission to minister only within your local church. In Baptist practice, you are licensed only at and through that church. Your license authorizes you to proclaim the word of God whenever a door of opportunity opens, but each church is autonomous. Your license is valid only while you are a member of the church where you received the license. If you move to another church, that new church may or may not recognize your license. As a licentiate minister, you are subject to the rules of that local pastor and church. You must conduct yourself in a manner that will honor the character of your congregation.

Question: What qualifies me for ordination?

Answer: In order to be considered for ordination, a licentiate minister must meet one or more of the following criteria:

- Receive the call to pastor an existing congregation.
- Receive the call to serve on the ministerial staff of an existing congregation.
- Receive the call to start a new church or mission.
- Receive the call to serve on the ministerial staff of a new church or mission.
- Receive the call to the mission field, either domestic or international.
- Complete an approved course of study taught by the pastor after the pastor has determined your readiness.
- Graduate from an accredited Bible college or seminary.

The English word "ordain" has three different meanings: to set in order, to establish, and to set apart for a special function. In common ecclesiastical usage ordination usually refers to special status accorded to ministers through officially sanctioned rites. These rites are primarily associated with the pastoral functions of proclaiming the Word of God and administering the sacraments of the Lord, but also include other priestly responsibilities such as performing marriages and committing the remains of the dead to the earth.

Chapter Six • *Answering the Call*

THE PREREQUISITES FOR ORDINATION

Although most branches of the Christian church ordain individuals who have received a public and formal call into the gospel ministry, the requirements for ordination differ from church to church. Broadly speaking, historically Christianity has sought to confirm three major prerequisites in the life of the candidate:

1. evidence of salvation;
2. evidence of a divine call or vocation; and
3. a formal call from a recognized New Testament ministry.

In the past, established ministries were limited to congregational pastoral ministries, chaplaincy in the armed forces or institutional settings, the office of evangelist, or service in a specific congregational ministry under the guidance of a senior pastor. In recent times, the New Testament church has grown into an organization requiring multiple staff positions. Today many congregations employ several ordained clergy persons. Positions such as youth ministers, Christian education ministers, and pastoral assistants have expanded ordination requirements and procedures.

Candidates for ordination should demonstrate sincere conviction and knowledge of the foundation doctrines of the denomination, especially in areas relevant to the specific ministry of calling. Normally the candidate is ordained in his or her own congregation, but occasional exceptions occur such as when the pastor and people of the congregation agree and recognize the need for ordination.

Expanded needs and ministry requirements have opened such new models of pastoral ministry as team ministry and associate pastors. Even as ministry explores new concepts and models, proper preparation remains essential. The church does not take ordination lightly. Ideally the stages of preparation are clearly defined and the abilities of the candidate carefully examined. Any individual truly called into the gospel ministry should have no objection to participating in a formal training process. Historically the call to minister includes the call to prepare. For the ordination candidate, training is a requirement, not an option.

Not everyone has the means to attend seminaries and major training academies, but other options abound. Church-operated Bible schools and institutes are among the many opportunities for training in the religious community. Regardless of the particular path chosen, every ordination candidate should participate in some form of professional training for the ministry.

Some churches require the candidate to write a statement of belief or spiritual autobiography outlining personal fundamentals of faith. Such a written statement is a helpful tool for the candidate who wishes to organize his or her thoughts. The document also allows members of the ordination council to prepare relevant questions for the formal examination.

Finally, personal character, ethics, and morals constitute areas of crucial concern. The ministry of the kingdom must remain a proving ground for righteousness. I cannot overemphasize the importance of strong moral fiber for those who answer the call to ministry in Christ's name. Ministry is a dual call into service. Primarily we serve God, and serving God demands that we serve the people of God. Both dimensions of ministry demand servants of impeccable integrity. The minister who proclaims one standard in the pulpit and lives by a lesser standard will inevitably forfeit the respect of the flock and bring shame upon the household of God.

> GOD'S CALLING ALONE IS ADEQUATE GROUNDS FOR MINISTRY

Ministry is an undertaking of eternal importance, and we must rigorously screen those who present themselves as candidates for this work Other professions have criteria for examining and determining the abilities of practitioners. Lawyers must pass the bar; physicians must pass a medical exam. Appropriate qualifying trials and examinations are an affirmation of the solemn responsibility of Christian ministry.

PREPARATION FOR ORDINATION COUNSEL AND INTERVIEW CALL

One's calling from God is intensely personal, but the church maintains the right to validate and confirm that calling through ordination. To this end the candidate must be prepared to explain and articulate the inward experience of calling through outward conversation with church leaders. God's calling alone is adequate grounds for ministry and you can add nothing to God's call. However, careful thought and reasoned preparation can help you defend your calling to others who must discern your readiness for ordination.

I offer the following checklists, questions, and resources to help prepare for interviews and conversations about the legitimacy of your call and your ability to do the work of the church. Do not use this chapter to figure out what interviewers want to hear. Instead, allow these pages to prompt your thinking so that you are not caught off-guard by any question. Give a thoughtful, honest accounting of yourself and leave the rest to God.

CALLING AND OPENNESS

- How would you share and articulate your calling to the ministry?
- What convictions led you to feel this call?
- Are you willing to go anywhere the Lord should lead?
- Does your spouse share your convictions?

SALVATION AND CHRISTIAN EXPERIENCE

- Are you ready to tell the story of your personal experience of salvation?
- How long have you been a Christian?
- How do the Scriptures support your claim to salvation?

DOCTRINE AND CHURCH

- What place does the Bible have in your ministry?
- How would you explain the doctrine of the Trinity?
- What is a call?
- Can you name books you have read dealing with doctrine?
- Can you list the Bible ordinances of the church?
- Who is the head of the church?

EDUCATIONAL GOALS AND VISION

- Have you had any experiences in Christian work? If so, what?
- What efforts have you made toward educational preparation for ministry?
- What are your future plans for education and ministry preparation?
- How will you make a difference in the Christian ministry?

Chapter Six • *Answering the Call*

Most Frequently Asked Questions and Answers

Question: Can a licentiate minister perform weddings and funerals?

Answer: A licentiate minister may not officiate a wedding or sign a state-issued marriage license. However, a licentiate may participate in a funeral or memorial service as designed by their pastor or may officiate alone at the service.

Question: What about participation in worship services?

Answer: As an associate minister at the church where you regularly worship and hold membership, your first responsibility is to be an integral part of the worship experience there. As such, whenever you are not preaching at another church, a mission, or prison, you should be present at worship. Do not neglect the weekly Bible study period and Sunday School. Do not avoid or resent pastoral guidance, but earnestly seek opportunities to learn from your pastor's experience. Do not make excuses to serve as a Sunday School, Bible School or Vacation Bible School teacher.

Attendance at all worship services is the stepping stone for a closer walk with God for both parishioners and ministers. How can anyone serve as a spiritual leader when absent from the congregation? Active participation at weddings, funerals, worship services, baptisms, Communions, revivals, and conferences creates a bond between the people and the minister. We must be there to share the joyful as well as the sad times with those who seek words of encouragement and inspiration.

> THE MORE WE GIVE GOD TO WORK WITH, THE MORE GOD MAKES OF US.

Question: What about education?

Answer: In Paul's second letter to Timothy, he instructs Timothy to "study to show yourself approved unto God, a workman that needs not be ashamed, who rightly divides the word of truth." This charge is for all Christians and especially for those called to the gospel ministry. Just as we expect our medical doctors and lawyers to be fully trained and educated, the people of God are worthy of the same level of expertise. We must provide the waiting congregation with the same level of competence.

Yes, the Holy Spirit guides and directs the faithful minister, but the more we give God to work with, the more God makes of us. A soldier of Christ must prepare for full-fledged work in God's kingdom. To serve God as ably as possible, we should further our education to the highest possible level. There are schools, Bible colleges, and seminaries in most cities. Consult your pastor for advice, scholarship information, and ministry emphasis before making final choices for your education.

Question: Do I need to purchase anything?

Answer: Yes. Purchase a robe. Make sure you have one outfit in which you will feel proud to serve the Lord. (See guidelines for proper dress earlier in this book.)

Begin to build a personal library immediately. As a starting point, consider these titles and topics:

- Concordance
- Bible Dictionary
- Bible Encyclopedia
- Bible Handbook
- Hermeneutics
- <u>Baptist Standard Church Directory and Busy Pastor's Guide</u>
- <u>Preaching Through a Storm</u> by H. Beecher Hicks, Jr.
- <u>The Image of the Black Preacher</u> by H. Beecher Hicks, Jr.
- <u>Black Preaching</u> by Henry H. Mitchell
- <u>Celebration and Experience in Preaching</u> by Henry

H. Mitchell
- Jesus and the Disinherited by Howard Thurman
- Design for Preaching by Henry Grady Davis
- God of the Oppressed by James Cone
- The Ministry Gifts by Kenneth Hagin
- Christian Ministers Guide from Standard Publishing
- Principles and Practices for Baptist Churches by Edward T. Hiscox

7

PRACTICAL MATTERS

LEADERSHIP AND PROFESSIONAL CONDUCT

A newly baptized Christian may believe he has arrived at the destination when he has actually just begun the journey of discipleship. By the same token, ordination and licensing does not complete God's calling, but only prepares the minister to pursue that calling in earnest. So far, we have addressed matters related to preparing and seeking ordination.

Now we will turn our attention to questions of practical service and courtesy that arise after ordination. A brief review of responsibilities and expectations will help novice ministers conduct themselves with assurance and confidence in the practice of church leadership.

A time of prayer precedes each worship service. All ministers should participate and arrive on time. Please come and pray with us; do not take a seat downstairs waiting for us. Even if you intend to sit in the balcony, in the pew, or with your family, please come to prayer before the service. Praying and worshiping together is the first step in fellowship and cooperation among leaders. We do not focus on personal matters or conduct business during this time. Instead we strive to become one in the Spirit through prayer.

The minister who does not come for prayer will not participate in the worship service or receive a pulpit assignment. Ushers, choirs, and deacons abide by these guidelines for prayerful preparation before worship and no lesser standard is acceptable for ministers.

Many ministers never attend Fellowship Services with the church, thereby neglecting an opportunity to support the pastor and church. The Fellowship Services also afford an occasion to build a network by meeting other ministers and pastors. Do not be selective, attending events only at large churches. Rural areas and small churches also have pressing needs, and God may call you to such service if you are present and available.

Attend weekly Bible class, both for your growth and as a model for others.

Be diligent in attending funerals, revivals, prayer breakfasts, workshops, and retreats. Seize every opportunity to serve. God may use such an event to bring your gifts to the attention of those seeking a minister.

Be as faithful in your ministry as you would if you were the pastor. Be faithful and one day you will be ruler. All day Sunday belongs to the Lord's service, not just a few hours. Occasionally you will have some important outside commitment on Sunday, but avoid chronic distractions and competitions on Sunday. Make ministry and service the highest priority of the day.

Chapter Seven • *Practical Matters*

Support the Monthly Ministers Fellowship by paying your dues and participating actively. The benefits will become clear for those who take part in the meetings.

Most Frequently Asked Questions and Answers

Question: If I am married, how should my spouse serve?

Answer: In most churches there are organizations and ministries through which your spouse can participate actively in the church. Seek classes and discussions that will assist the spouse in growing as a Christian, cultivating a ministry of support, and offering a role model. If such opportunities are absent, consider putting your spouse in charge as the leader or advisor of such a group. Your spouse must make every effort to assist you in growth and development.

Question: What is my role when I sit in the pulpit?

Answer: As spiritual leaders, we receive the respect of the congregation. One who respected must also be respectful. "To whom much is given, much is required." The congregation studies our actions in the pulpit. Slouching, eating, and playing are distracting and detrimental to the worship experience. The congregation has come to lay its needs before God. They are looking for the Lord to minister to them through our leadership in worship. We must never take for granted the sacred trust granted us as representatives of God's healing grace. Always be mindful of the image one projects to the congregation. What does the worshiper see when looking upon you or me?

Question: What is appropriate pulpit attire?

Answer: On the first Sunday at our church the normal pulpit attire for licensed and ordained ministers is a basic black robe that zips up the front, preferably with dark attire beneath the robe. Additionally, ministers wear robes for all Communion services. Navy blue, black or dark suits represent acceptable attire for all other Sundays or weekday services that do not include Communion. The attire for evening services during revivals and conferences is nicely pressed suits of any reasonable color. Admittedly, this practice varies in different congregations. Some pastors expect ministers to wear robes every Sunday, while others require associate ministers to don a robe only when preaching. Know and respect the policy in your congregation.

Question: What about serving in the balcony or the overflow or other assignments?

Answer: As an associate minister, the pastor may call upon you to serve in various areas according to the needs of the moment. No assignment is too large to undertake or too small to perform with dignity and diligence. Persons worshiping in the overflow have every right as to have the physical presence of one of God's ambassadors present with them. After the preached word, the minister in the balcony and ministers in the pulpit will move down the aisle with extended arms of invitation. The ministers serving in the overflow will also invite persons to come to Christ as the pastor does so in the main sanctuary. Also, while serving in the overflow, you will pray with and for worshipers in your area during the altar call. Any associate minister seated in the pulpit or in the reserved minister's seating is eligible for immediate service. Assignments are not negotiable. If asked to serve, report to that area quickly and with a right spirit, ready to serve the people of God.

Question: If I am late for worship, may I quietly "slip" into the pulpit?

Answer: Absolutely not. You may never enter the pulpit late. Our promptness sets an example for the congregation.

Question: Now that I am a minister, am I expected to tithe?

Answer: Yes. All ministers should tithe. Tithing is an act of faith and trust in the God who calls you to preach and teach His word. Being in a leadership role requires us to live up to the highest standards.

Question: Does my license to preach allow me to give pastoral counseling?

Answer: Associate ministers should not counsel in the name of the church unless given a direct mandate from the pastor. The Bible says that the pastor is the shepherd and "watches for the souls" of those ministers. If you become aware of difficulties or concerns among members, inform the pastor. When given permission to counsel with troubled members, encourage them to speak to their pastor as well, even if only briefly. Explain clearly that you will report to the pastor that you are counseling a member. Most pastors will not need to know the specifics of the counseling sessions, notifying the pastor shows proper respect. In all circumstances we must take great care to assure that our counsel is strictly the word of God.

Question: If I am asked to preach at another church, do I need the pastor's permission?

Answer: Yes. Courtesy requires you to inform the pastor. Invite the pastor to read or review your sermon. If there are any reservations, please be open to your pastor's counsel.

Question: Are the ministers expected to pray together each Sunday morning?

Answer: Yes. Prayer is the final preparation for worship. The pastor, pulpit assistants and all ministers normally pray prior to the worship service. Invoking God's presence and power before worship brings everyone on one accord. Some churches have prayer ministries offering intercession during the worship services. Associate ministers who participate in this group will develop and grow in their prayer life.

Question: Who determines which ministers sit in the pulpit?

Answer: A pulpit assistant makes these assignments at the request of the Pastor after the need for a minister is communicated.

The assignments are random and the pastor makes every effort to delegate assignments fairly among all the associate ministers.

GUIDELINES FOR VISITATION

Associate ministers are Christians first and calling on the sick or troubled is part of our Christian responsibility. Keep in mind the follow guidelines for visitation.

Home Visitation

- Never go alone!

Hospital Visitation

- Inquire at the nurse's station regarding any restrictions or special instructions relevant to your visit.
- Do not make contact with any bodily fluids.
- Wash your hands thoroughly after completing your visit.
- Share the word of God, not bad news or gossip.
- Minister through prayer, Scripture, or song.
- Unless circumstances are exceptional, stay no longer than ten to fifteen minutes.

Nursing Home Visitation

- Minister to the need of the patient.
- Share the word of God, not bad news or gossip.
- Minister through prayer, Scripture, or song.
- Normally stay no longer than ten to fifteen minutes.

Prison

- Take the word of God with you.

- Witness and evangelize.
- Do not give out personal information.
- Do not make promises that you cannot fulfill once the person has been released.

Hospice and Terminally Ill Visitation

- Speak words of comfort.
- Share the word of God through prayer and Scripture.
- Share the assurances of God.

BEREAVEMENT MINISTRY

As ministers of Jesus Christ, our living Lord, we are privileged to bear His comfort to those in sorrow. Upon learning of a death, go immediately to the family. Late in life, William E. Sweeney reflected, "It was not what I said that helped, but that I went, and that by going showed I cared."

When death occurs in a hospital, spend a few moments alone with the family. Most hospitals have rooms for this purpose.

This is no time to be talkative. Simple words of comfort suffice. Whether quoted from memory or read aloud, Scripture is always appropriate. Even if a grieving family doesn't ask you to pray, you should offer. You may say, "I'd like to have prayer. May we do that?" The bereaved will nearly always appreciate the offer.

Show your sensitivity to the family by being there, listening, and feeling their sorrow with them. Spend as much time as will be helpful without intruding upon their need for privacy. When you leave, remind the family members that you will be as near as the telephone. If you make that promise, you must be earnest in keeping it. If you must leave the office, be sure the secretary or volunteer knows how to reach you.

After the family has made arrangements with the funeral home, the funeral director will call you regarding the hour for the service. Death takes precedence. If at all possible, adjust your schedule to accommodate the time best suited to the family.

In their sorrow, the family may request visitation or solace from another minister with whom they are close. The local minister should graciously convey this request to his colleague, making every effort to cooperate on the details of the service.

When a family bypasses the local minister entirely, he should still call on the family as a gesture of sympathy. His gracious manner will indicate that he understands their need and that he feels no hurt or resentment because they have not asked him to participate.

You may call on the family again the day before the funeral or during visitation hours at the funeral home to ask, "Is there a favorite Scripture or the words of a particular song you would like included in the service?"

If they have no requests, you could reply, "I'd like to use the 23rd Psalm, 'The Lord is my shepherd….'" By referring to Scripture, you help mourners focus their thoughts upon God and His presence.

You may also want to ask, "Is there a friend or family member you would like to say a few words?"

Including a family member or friend helps to personalize the service even more. However, the eulogy should neither supplant nor detract from the minister's remarks regarding the deceased.

Discuss the details of the service with the funeral director. Clarify details about time and place. Should there be singing? An obituary? Will there be a fraternal or military service? Does the church provide pallbearers? In what section of the funeral home will the service be held? Where does the minister wait? Where does he stand for his message? How will the body be loaded into the funeral coach, and will the minister precede the body? Will he drive his own car to the grave or ride with the funeral director? What is the procedure at the cemetery? Ask all questions before the service begins. No one wants confusion or surprises at such an emotional event.

On the day of the service, if pallbearers carry the body to the waiting funeral coach, the minister precedes them, walking slowly as the casket is carried and standing near as it is loaded into the hearse. After the service, the minister will again lead the casket as it is borne to the waiting funeral coach. Clear communication between the funeral director and the officiating minister insures a smooth and orderly service.

Funeral customs vary from congregation to congregation and in different localities. If in doubt, the following order of worship offers a practical guide for planning the home going service.

- Organ background of selected hymns
- Singing (optional)
- Scripture reading
- Prayer
- Obituary (optional)
- Remarks by family members or friends (optional)
- Message
- Closing prayer and benediction
- Soft organ music as friends and family leave

Make the funeral message personal without becoming maudlin. Strive to alleviate rather than increase the family's sorrow. The entire service, unless there is singing, requires no more than twenty minutes.

CONCLUSION

THE VERDICT

THE WORD OF THE JUDGE

The subject of church etiquette could fill many books. I hope this volume will serve as a practical introduction for church leaders and members. I commend this guide for use in new member orientation, classes, youth groups, and other training programs in the local churches.

Many businesses have slogans promising customer satisfaction. Some feel the church should adopt a similar stance. However, even the company striving to please the customer has guidelines to follow.

In the church, our ultimate guideline is the Word of God. Our first responsibility is not to please one another, but to please our Lord. Therefore, orderly and respectful behavior is the goal among God's people. In our eagerness to "be treated right" we too often trample on one another. In the end, no one is treated right as long as we believe the world owes us something. Only when we focus upon what we owe God will we find our way to order, respect, and courtesy in the church.

> OUR ULTIMATE GUIDELINE IS THE WORD OF GOD.

Make certain your church has a program or system to train worshipers on how they should behave. Members cannot follow standards they don't know about. Perhaps church members have never been adequately trained concerning church etiquette. Strive to model proper behavior during and after worship. When people know better, they do better.

GENTLE GUIDANCE

We must be cautious in how we correct individuals who are out of order in the church. Temper correction with the patience and love of God. We find a biblical example in the gentleness of Aquila and Priscilla in the story from Acts 18. This couple offers us a model for correcting Christian behavior and, in this case, Christian doctrine. Like the apostle Paul, Aquila and Priscilla were tentmakers by trade, yet they also had a much higher calling as committed and concerned church members. A powerful preacher named Apollos came to the attention of Aquila and Priscilla. The Alexandrian Apollos was eloquent, mighty in Scriptures, instructed in the way of the Lord, fervent in the Spirit, and diligently in teaching. In spite of his many gifts, Apollos had a deficient understanding of baptism. When Aquila and Priscilla heard Apollos teach, they did not openly criticize his errors. They did not elevate themselves at Apollos' expense. Instead, the compassionate couple called Apollos aside and privately corrected his misunderstanding. This sainted couple expounded or explained to Apollos the way of God more perfectly. Was he convinced because of their message? Yes, the message of Jesus Christ will always save. Was he convinced because of their approach and method? Yes, yes, and yes again.

This guidebook is intended to instruct the reader in love. I have sought to avoid a technical or theological approach in favor of presenting a practical guide for church members. I invite teachers and students into a mutual dialogue as the reading of this guide leads to meaningful discussion on matters we have merely touched upon in these chapters. After reading these pages, I pray that when you find an "Apollos", you will take him or her aside and expound on the way of the Lord and His church in a loving and exciting way.

ABOUT THE AUTHOR

The Reverend Dr. William E. Flippin, Sr. is a native of Nashville, Tennessee. His parents, Virginia and Richard Flippin recognized his leadership ability early in his childhood and encouraged him to succeed through education. He graduated with honors from Pearl High School in Nashville, where he served as president of the student body during his senior year. He furthered his education and earned a Bachelor of Arts degree in Mathematics and Business Administration from Fisk University in Nashville, graduating in 1974. In addition, he holds a Master of Divinity degree (Cum Laude) from Candler School of Theology at Emory University in Atlanta, Georgia; and a Doctorate of Ministry from McCormick Theological Seminary in Chicago, Illinois.

Among his many accomplishments, Dr. Flippin has distinguished himself by being named a Benjamin E. Mays Scholar for three years at Emory University; an inductee of the Morehouse College Board of Distinguished Preachers. He is on the Board of Trustees for the Morehouse School of Religion.

Faithfully serving as Senior Pastor of The Greater Piney Grove Baptist Church in Atlanta since 1990, Pastor Flippin has led Greater Piney Grove to a unique sense of mission and outreach. The church has grown to a membership of over 7,000 people. Each Sunday, three morning worship services speak of this pastor's vision for "equipping the saints." In his pastoral ministry, he has licensed and ordained over forty ministers and deacons. Under his leadership, Dr. Flippin has added a staff to develop programs of fulltime ministry that serves the community and the world. In the fall of 1996, a multipurpose Family Life Center with more than 25,000 square feet of space was completed. This modern facility houses a gymnasium, child development center, bookstore, library, conference room and classrooms and is valued at almost $2,000,000. Reverend Flippin and The Greater Piney Grove family has also purchased over 30 acres of land for ministry expansion. The project is called 'The Promised Land.'

Dr. Flippin has been a pastor with distinction for two other historic churches in Georgia: Springfield Baptist Church, Greensboro, from 1980 – 1986; and Shoal Creek Baptist Church, Locust Grove, from 1986 – 1990. Occasionally, Pastor Flippin serves as visiting professor at Beulah Heights Bible College and Luther Rice Seminary. Dr. Flippin has had the honor of delivering the Baccalaureate Sermons at Fisk University (Nashville) and at Morehouse College (Atlanta).

Having a strong sense of community, Dr. Flippin serves on several community action committees and boards. In 1982, Dr. Flippin became an Associate in the Department of Black Church Relations for the Georgia Baptist Convention. His primary role was to relate and establish joint cooperative religious activities between black and white Baptists in Georgia. In 1990, he was appointed to serve as a consultant for the convention and administers the Durward V. Cason Scholarship, which has a corpus of over $200,000. Additionally, Dr. Flippin serves as Board Chairman for Higher Plain Community Development, Incorporated, focusing on issues facing children and women in an economically diverse community.

He is the Board Chairman and CEO for The Pearl Initiative, Inc and The Pearls of Great Price Ministries. Dr. Flippin has been appointed by two Georgia Governors to serve on various state commissions. He was a delegate, from Dekalb County, to the National Democratic Party. He also serves as instructor for the National Baptist Congress of Christian Education; member of the Dekalb Chapter 100 Black Men; lifetime member of Alpha Phi Alpha Fraternity, Incorporated; and lifetime member of the NAACP. He conducts motivational and leadership workshops throughout the country and has traveled extensively to the Middle East while continuing to direct several programs that have allowed Baptists in Georgia to work together successfully.

Dr. Flippin has been married for almost thirty years to Sylvia Taylor, who is a high school mathematics instructor. Mrs. Flippin is a graduate of Vanderbilt University in Nashville and holds a Master's degree in Education from Georgia State University. For over ten years, Mrs. Flippin has taught in the Ministers' Wives Division for the National Baptist Congress of Christian Education and is an active member of Alpha Kappa Alpha Sorority.

Dr. and Mrs. Flippin are the proud parents of three sons and a daughter. William, Jr. is an ordained minister, a graduate of Morehouse College, Class of 1998 and a graduate of the Interdenominational Theological Center (ITC) with a Masters of Divinity degree. Recently, he received his Master of Theology degree from Candler School of Theology at Emory University in Atlanta, Ga. In the fall of 2003, William will be pursuing his Ph.D. at Lutheran Theological Seminary in Chicago concentrating in Church History and Reformation Studies.

Richard (Ricky) Curtis, is a graduate of Morehouse College, Class of 2001. He is a third year student at Candler School of Theology at Emory. He is also an ordained minister. For the past two summers, Richard has been the Summer Academy minister at Morehouse College. He will serve in this capacity in the summer of 2004.

Continuing the heritage, Joseph Charles Taylor, an ordained minister, is a recent Cum Laude graduate of Morehouse College, Class of 2003, with a Bachelor of Arts degree in Political Science and Sociology. In the fall of 2003, Joseph will be attending Wesley Theological Seminary with a full scholarship.

Their daughter, Sylvia Joi, is a high school senior in the Fulton County School System and sings in the Greater Piney Grove Youth Choir.